I0146892

LIVING IN THE
GREY MATTERS

LIVING IN THE GREY MATTERS

By Tracey L. Pagana

Copyright © *2022* Tracey L. Pagana
All rights reserved.
ISBN - 979-8-218-07367-1

BOOKS BY TRACEY L. PAGANA

Innerspace

If You Could Choose From My Cup

Slow Dancing with Silence

Coming Out Of Darkness

Living In The Grey Matter

DEDICATION

To all the light workers who support each other in the many capacities of unconditional love. Without the team that combines our working efforts to unite source we would not be capable of completing our loving mission of educational wisdom. The constant flow of loving, living energy surrounding unconditional love. I am grateful for my team I am in awe and gratitude for the cause and effects that seems to multiply in strength our team works together in. May you all find this love and light to feed and guide you.

THANK YOU

I thank every person who continues to grow with me on this journey for always being at the right place at the right time to manifest the magic of getting this work into the world. Thank you Laurie Smydo for the amazing cover art and all the fabulous contributions you made to get this book complete. Thank you Wendy Trumbley and Maria Webb for contributing your unique gifts to this work.

Thank you to my wonderful partner Joe who steps aside and lets me write this message for source so we can all grow independently while supporting each other. Thank you Divine Source for continuing to teach us how to grow and evolve the world into Divine light.

FOREWORD

It's funny, I have always had a saying that I "live in the grey zone" when it comes to life. Some people live in 'black and white', but I was always more comfortable in the grey. What I mean by this is that although I am, by nature, a rule follower, I am not someone who can live in a world where there aren't exceptions to the rules. I am comfortable with people going against the grain if that is what is ultimately best for their personal growth or needs.

When my dear friend Tracey asked me to write the forward for this book and then explained the premise to me, I had to laugh because what I had been saying in jest my whole life ran deeper and truer than I could have ever imagined.

By trade, I have a psychology and sociology background, so I know about grey matter in the brain and how it naturally begins to thin out as we age. By blessing, I am also very aware of my soul's connection to Spirit/Source/Home and have seen brain scans done on those who identify as Mediums, in which the grey matter of the brain, primarily the frontal lobe, lights up during moments when the medium is channeling spirit, showing that somehow this matter in the brain links humans to Spirit/Source/Home. I am a person who loves evidence and proof and scientific measure, but I am not naïve or closed minded enough to discount that which cannot be explained by science – faith, miracles and psychic phenomena.

My own understanding of grey matter and connection with all things Spirit/Home comes from my childhood journey through personal struggle and loneliness. *I* call it Home because a) that is where I feel and know in my soul, we come from and where we return to and b) it is my greatest source of comfort and inner peace.

My journey with grey zones:

Before I begin, I must clarify something. Home life for me, as a child was tumultuous, but it was not bereft of love and good times. My parents, although lacking in compassion and tact much of the time, were doing the best they could be based on the era in which they were raised and the time period in which they were raising kids. My childhood took place in a period of time when therapy and unpacking our baggage wasn't a thing. Where being healthy didn't include mental health and involved cigarettes, whiskey, and boxed wine as part of one's diet! So, although my childhood picture may seem dismal at times, I am ultimately highlighting the forces and situations that led me to work with my grey matter and spirit.

As a child, I was raised by a stay-at-home mother who loved her children and made them her life. An often-self-righteous woman who had fleeting friendships because she could not see past the flaws of others as she was so insecure about her own. Her very own flaws, especially her lack of mercy, her lack of friendships, made her dependent upon her children to feed her emotional needs. This was an impossible and emotionally draining task for her kids.

My father on the other hand, was a physical laborer who did not raise us at all. He only disciplined us; a 1950's vision of discipline, physical based punishment. My father was a business owner and work-a-holic out of financial and pride-based necessity. After 12-hour days, he would drink himself into relaxation only to drive home to eat dinner with his family and berate us for anything we had upset our mother with that day. If he didn't berate us, he would start verbally picking at my mother, who fought back with insults that were equal in hurt, but who also relied on us to defend her and try to calm our father down. Sometimes my parents would wait until we were in bed before fighting, leaving us too nervous to come out of our rooms in our mother's defence and even more afraid that they were going to get divorced.

The emotional instability within the house kept all of us in line and good as gold. We never talked back, unless defending our mother's honour, even then, we were never disrespectful. We always did as we were told. We used our manners. We apologized for everything. We learned to ignore what was best for us if it meant not disappointing adults. Understanding others boundaries was ingrained in us. Setting them for ourselves was not a luxury that children were privy to in our house.

When it came to a religious or Godly influence as children, we did not have a healthy one. I always felt grateful or blessed for everything I had. I understood that other people had it far worse than I did. As a kid I didn't connect this gratitude to an entity, I just knew that I felt grateful. My father taught Sunday school until my oldest sister was in JK, at which point he resigned from this role because he did not agree with his church's new mandate on tithing. My parents could barely afford their mortgage and food let alone an expected donation of wages to their church every month. After this resignation, my parents were hurt and never encouraged their children to form a relationship with God. Instead, my father's anger towards the institution of religion that *he* knew, became one of his weapons towards us in times of disapproval when he would yell at us over something that upset him, the table being set wrong, a phrase we may use, wanting to use the car to which he would yell that we should read the Bible or that we were a disgrace because we didn't know the Bible. Our lack of religious upbringing became OUR fault. Any argument had with him would somehow lead him into bigoted epithets that he would link to Biblical and religious values as a means of proving *our* liberal or forward thinking incorrect. This only led us to question if we even wanted to be a part of the very 'Thing' he kept faulting us for. Why would I want to believe in or follow something that seemed so judgmental and exclusive?

I was emotionally mature for my age based on my forced emotional/mental maturity in the home and had developed a sarcastic sense of humour (not harsh, but funny) as a defence mechanism. Being funny meant people didn't suspect I was depressed or drowning in responsibility and guilt for not being able to save/help/fix those I was responsible for.

Around people, I was what you would describe as "quirky." I called *everyone* my friend, whether I had just met them or sat next to them since first grade, but I didn't actually have friends that I played with, hung out with, slept over with, or talked to outside of class with, not until high school. Kids didn't want to play with me at recess or have me over to their house save for maybe two kids throughout elementary school. It was easier for them to target and mock me than it was for them to try to understand or get to know me.

My childhood relationships with peers involved kids defacing playground equipment with rude words about me, food being thrown at me, teasing, bullying, exclusion from peer groups and psychosomatic symptoms that left me with blinding migraines. By grade 8, I developed situational depression.

I never told my parents about the bullying because I didn't want to stress them out any more than they already were and certainly didn't need them thinking I was a 'loser' or 'weird' too. By the end of grade 8, I went and sat at a park by myself and pulled out a bottle of over-the-counter pills, determined I was going to take the bottle, walk home and just go to bed. I got 10 in and a voice in my head *(that wasn't mine)* told me 'You *can't* do this'. So, without even second guessing it, I stopped, went home and never talked about it until right now. In high school life got better socially but started off with me being held at fake gun point, while working alone at night in a local store. I didn't know the gun was fake and I didn't really know the kid behind it. I was alone in the store. I panicked and cried like a child *(because I was a child)*. I never told a soul for years. The kid felt bad, told me it was joke and then bragged about it to his friends at school.

Trust didn't come easy. I never learned to let others help me or take care of me.

THIS was my childhood and adolescence. The understated experiences above, led me to question the existence of a God, Heaven, Angels, or anything that might save me or provide release in my life.

Growing up, I had no idea I was surviving trauma. I thought I was lucky that I had food, a house, a bed to sleep in and clothes. Don't get me wrong, I was lucky to have those blessings, and I lacked the second tier of Maslow's Hierarchy of needs, security. Looking back as an adult, I could see that I lacked this sense of security in my relationships, but what I was also able to see was that Source/Spirit, tried to provide me with security and love through connecting with my grey matter.

Here's how:

From the time I was 6 *(at least this is my first memory of it)*, I was terrified to be alone or in the dark, especially at night once everyone else was asleep. I could fall asleep before the others in my house, but I would always wake up late at night and be paralyzed by fear. I would see shadows going across my bedroom doorway, see random lights flickering in the hall, feel a wave of cold press against my cheek or lie beside me, feel hands or something weighted tap along the mattress as I lie on it, hear voices that I could never quite make out, talking in my basement, etc.

I would call for my mother and she would let me sleep on her floor – *because under the bed beside wasn't terrifying as well?!* My mother would tell me "It was nothing," that I was "making it up" or "ghosts aren't real" as a way of helping me understand that what I was seeing/hearing, wasn't really there and there was nothing to be afraid of. In her defence, it wasn't real for her! She couldn't see it or hear it.

By 8 years old, anytime I was alone or going to bed, I started the habit of talking out loud, begging whatever was there to "please don't show yourself to me. I don't want to turn around and see someone standing there. It will scare me, and I don't want to be scared." I would then try to appease *them* by saying, "if you need me to know something or see something, please just show it to me in my head so I don't have to see it jump out at me." This actually seemed to work for me after a while. I would still hear a little girl singing out in the garage or have random things happen like objects fall in the other room, only to seemingly land in places that could not be explained away, but it was no longer happening right in front of my eyes. It wasn't any less scary for me since I had no clue what was going on and why it seemed to be "targeted" at me, but it was an internal coping mantra that seemed to give me some sense of control.

On top of "knowing" that something or someone was with me, I also found that I had a "knowing "of things that were to come. It often came about as fleeting thoughts that I dismissed as coincidence or chalked up to just knowing people well. For example, I would have a random thought or daydream about the teacher announcing a pop quiz, only to have it happen later that day or the next day; all things that could easily be explained away.

This was a constant in my life. My siblings never experienced it, but my sister would witness it from time to time while in my presence. I never liked being home alone because it never felt like I was *actually* alone. The noises or random voices or distant chatter that I would hear, scared me and made think I was going crazy. Even into my late 20's, I would frequently have night terrors and need my husband to bring me to consciousness during my episodes. I am sure at first, he thought I was possessed!

As a teenager, this phenomenon didn't stop, and it wasn't until my grandfather passed away that I connected any of this to God. At 17, I didn't know what I believed. I was questioning everything, especially God's existence. When my grandfather, whom I wasn't close with, passed away, I had a very vivid dream about him where we sat down and had a conversation and the only thing, he said to me was "It's real." I knew instantly what he meant. He was telling me that God and Heaven and Angels and all of it was real. I woke up and felt like I knew the answer to one of the greatest debates of all time, because I did! Weeks after this dream I went to visit my grandmother and although I thought nothing of the meaning behind the dream, I also felt a pressing need to tell her my dream. Her reaction was everything. My grandmother looked at me and wept. She told me that my grandfather went to church with her every Sunday with her for almost 50 years and he never believed in God. She told me that she was so worried about what would happen to his soul once he passed because in her church, she was taught that if you don't believe, you go to hell. She told me that my dream, my words, had brought her the peace that she needed and now she finally knew that her husband was with God in Heaven.

I had no clue at that time, which was the first message I would deliver from Spirit.

As a teen, I found solace in books by authors like Sylvia Browne or John Edwards. These books put my mind at ease about losing my mental faculties and also raised a world of questions for me as well. Why me? How was this even possible? Why were they scaring me? How could I even begin to make sense of the words when all I could hear was garbled chatter?

Looking back, my first moment with messages from spirit, was not my conversation with my grandmother, but rather when I was in grade 9, the year I finally made friends! After having spent what seemed like a lifetime without friends, praying for God (who I wasn't even sure existed) to send me someone who would understand me and love me for me, I was walking down the hallway at school and passed a very cute senior student. I have no clue what came over me, but I ran outside to where my friends were having lunch and I blurted out to them that I had just met the man that I was going to marry. I did not think anything of this since I was really just more infatuated with this boy's looks and only knew his name. Fast forward 4 years when I was a senior and he was a college graduate; we ended up working at Blockbuster together and dating. After 7 years of dating, we got married and had children. This boy/man got me. He understood what it was like to grow up in conflict and feel alone. We were very different, but we understood each other, we just got along. Always. I have no doubt that he was a gift to me. A piece of my peace that I had prayed for.

At the age of 29, I was blessed to meet a woman who saw this gift in me, this gift that I was so intrigued by and afraid of. She told me that my third eye was open and no matter how much I tried to close it, Spirit was right there and not going anywhere. She told me that if I just LISTENED to Spirit, made time to hear or see what they were trying to show me, that I would be able to work with them and learn to control it.

Sure! Piece of cake! HOW THE HECK DOES ONE DO THAT?!

This woman told me to set an hour aside before bed and just write down whatever came to my mind. She warned me to not worry about what I was writing, just write. So, I did. And the moment I started doing that, I stopped having nightmares and stopped being afraid to be home alone. At first, I would look at my writing and wonder, *"what have I been smoking?!!!"* But then I would Google parts of it and realize that it was actually factual information. It didn't always work this way, but the times it did, it made me feel better.

After this, my new mentor suggested I try reading people. She set up a workshop and I went to it. In this workshop she brought in a woman who passed around keys for people to hold to see what energy or information they could feel coming off of the keys. The moment she offered her items to the room, I was flooded with these horrible thoughts and started scribbling down what I was getting. I wrote down the following things: "Teen boy. Struggled. Deceased. This lady's son."

I was immediately appalled with myself for what I had written and could not bring myself to tell this woman this is what I saw. I mean, what if she had a son? I was not going to put that fear into her. I had kids, I could understand what that would feel like. When it was my turn to discuss what I got from this energy, I just used emotions to describe what I had gotten. "Heartbreak, loss, traumatic". The woman politely agreed with my assessment of the emotional energy and then told her story. She was a mother of 4 and her oldest was diagnosed with cancer at 11. He battled this horrid disease and lost. It was absolutely heart wrenching. She was sitting directly behind me as she talked and caught a glimpse of my paper with the appalling things. As I left workshop that day, my mentor and her friend chased me down and told me I was truly gifted and with more practice, I would be a sought-after source of connection one day.

Connecting with spirit gave me a peace I had never known or

understood. I slept better. My mindset was more positive. I felt my purpose and through this I started to feel my worth which meant I started to understand that setting boundaries was healthy and that I was worth speaking up for. It seemed to be a key to unlocking the path to self-love and acceptance for me.

I told my family what I could do, but never told those in my community or place of work. I didn't want anyone to judge me unfairly before getting to know me. My anonymity is and has always been kept even though I have read a great number of people. I live in a community and have a career that would not be as quick to understand this gift as those who are reading this book!

I started by doing readings for my mother's friends and my mentor's clients that she would send my way. My readings started out as 3 hr sessions because I didn't know how to pare down the information and get what was needed. Over time, sessions could be completed in 30 minutes to an hour and understanding the messages became easier and easier.

My husband was the most supportive in this. He didn't understand it. I'm not sure I fully did at first either, but he was understanding of my needs and knew it was a missing piece to my puzzle that seemed to complete me just a little bit more. After a few years of reading people and travelling to their houses so that my children weren't around making noise, my husband built me my own space to do my readings. A space for meditation and a zone for me to connect with spirit and maintain the privacy of my client.

Even after our marriage ended, my husband remained my person. Our separation only further proved to me he was a blessing of solace in my life. We held each other's hand through our split and wanted nothing but the best in life for one another. He gets me and understands my quirkiness. He has never judged me for trauma I have experienced or the side of me that can't be fully explained by science. He has always supported this gift in me and together we support it in our children.

With our daughters, I began to witness in them, what I went through as a child. They would go in spurts of waking up every night for 3 weeks at a time, scared because someone was talking to them, or they had a bad dream that they couldn't quite explain. I never told them "It's not real, go back to bed." Instead, I taught them that "sometimes spirit forgets that it's bedtime for us and that we need to sleep" and then I would get them to say a prayer that I made up so that they would be heard. The prayer worked for them, they could add what they wanted to it, but the base prayer went like this:

"Now I lay me down to sleep. I pray the Lord my soul to keep. God bless (insert names of family here). Lord, please surround me with the white light of the Holy Spirit and the Golden light of the Lord. Please take away my negative cell memory and help me get a good night's sleep. No spirits or ghosts in my room tonight, only Angels to help me sleep".

If ever I found them up late chatting to themselves, I would pop my head in and ask them who they were talking to. They're answers were always my favourite: "My Friend Deacon, Mom!", "Great Grandfather", "The Up and Downs". I never actually knew who or what they were referring to, but I would always tell them, "Okay! Please tell them that you have to go to bed now, but they are welcome to come back during the daytime when you are awake!" Sometimes, my kids would look right passed me and talk to someone over my shoulder *(which is never really a settling feeling!)*, then say their goodbyes and go to bed. My main goal was for them to understand that there is a beautiful situation that is MUCH bigger than us that we cannot fully explain, but also that setting boundaries for yourself is healthy and important – whether you are a child or adult. I also wanted them to understand that sometimes we are only scared of these things because our soul and brain forget to connect – our soul knows this all to be real, but our brain is hard wired to our bodies and gets confused because it doesn't know how to process the supernatural without greater understanding of it. So, I try to help them with the greater understanding and acceptance of what we cannot explain.

As my kids get older, I see how they are connected and how spirit communicates through them. They don't quite understand what they are doing when they give messages or know things and that's perfect because they still have a ton of human learning to do first! The soul comes here for growth and if it spends too much time, especially in childhood, connected to its Home, it can be harder for it to form connections and experiences on Earth. Balance is key with all things in life.

When I look back on my childhood now, knowing what I know about Spirit and our ability to connect with Heaven… HOME. I know that God/Angels/Spirits were providing me with a connection to my soul's Home that I was not getting while living in my earthly home. They were trying to give me the comfort I needed to go on in this lifetime. Because my soul and brain were already starting to separate their spiritual connection and begin the transition away from the soul's spiritual roots in Heaven in order to live this life on earth, my brain was not recognizing these signs as comfort, rather it was viewing it as a threat.

At the time, I didn't realize God was recognizing my soul was lonely and was providing it with company; just like I didn't realize He was sending me a clear message that He would be sending me one of "my people" that would get me and support me in ways I could not imagine I would need. Had I read biblical parables and stories as a child, I may have connected that in our darkest times God never forsakes us, he sends us messages/messengers of hope and lets us know He is there. He sends us what we need to help us through. He did just that for me. I truly believe that even though I married and divorced my person, that his soul came to me for the duration of this lifetime and that is why we remain the best of friends still.

Through my grey matter experience, God was providing me with the foundation to have the faith in Goodness that I needed and this faith in turn showed me the Goodness in *me* and helped me understand who I was. Once I saw I was worthy of love and kindness, I expected those things.

My journey through all of this brought me to Tracey and her

beautiful gift of healing the soul and helping it feel its worth. From the moment she embraced me with a hug that made me feel like I was Home and in the presence of Mother God, my soul began to align with all the work it had been processing for years. I had already begun my healing and connection with Source, but it wasn't until after working with Tracey that I was able to truly feel my worth and set my own boundaries – allowing me to shine brighter and meet the potential my soul held in store for me.

For Tracey, I will be forever grateful. She is truly a shepherd of Light and Love, bringing those she connects with through the night and into the sunrise. Thank you for your sharing your beautiful gift my friend. Thank you for being a blessing in my life. Thanking you for helping me to enhance my grey matter's connection to source!

-    *EM*

TABLE OF CONTENTS

Having a Voice Matters

Loving From the Centre of Your Heart

The Power of Grey Grace

The Quiet World of Grey

What Do You Do With All The Free Space?

Living In the Moment Matters

LIVING IN THE
GREY MATTERS

We cannot grow what we do not know and we do not know what we cannot grow. This mantra of describing life for me has been rumbling around my head a lot lately. Like the tumbleweeds and mini sand tornados rolling across the expanse of the Mexican mountains; this wind has a mind of its own, searching for spaces yet to be discovered, looking to settle in the desert landscape that encompasses me. As I witness this natural, daily occurrence in my unfamiliar environment, I cannot help thinking about the practice of this mantra. Reminding myself that this essence, this wind, this energy, is the same for me. I am searching deeper within, looking to settle, take root and discover new ground to break through. A place to sharpen my spiritual tools and a place to grow then. A place to discover and uncover the grey matter I choose to find balance in.

It is a beautiful Monday morning, on the very last day of January 2022 and the winds are very intense. Looking out I see the beautiful scenic view of the mountain that surrounds us on both sides. The circles of wind are increasing in numbers. As the dust settles, and filters in, the window cracks are aligned with the sun beams, visible and thick. There is a fine layer of dust that happens here daily and sprinkles its existence on my counters, floors, and tables. I am told that for the first three months of the year here, it is just the way it is in the middle of the Mexican mountains. On this day, the colour of grey in the air is a result of the granular sand mixing with the wind and the strength it carries.

We are gradually easing ourselves into the idea of retirement, after many years of investing ten to twelve hours a day in our active work life, for five days a week, and sometimes more than that. I have had a challenging time adjusting to the feeling of quiet and slow deliberation in our new home. It is an eerie feeling I am experiencing. Watching Joe settle in to this new, quiet routine and space while I struggle with the feeling of not yet completing something important. As a result, this space has amplified the energy for me and the feeling I need to be more productive.

The quiet is louder with two people finding a new routine to which they are not yet accustomed. Here, gone is the structure of our previously familiar day in and day out work/life routine. Where our working hours were constant and filled with meetings or appointments. Creating balance and order daily. Without a plan on how to fill our days in Mexico, the guilt for me is like the fine grey grit the wind carries and covers your things, body and space; both internally and externally.

Retirement, for me, is a concept that requires marinating in the process, like a long simmering stew. You plan for it, you dream about it, and when it starts to peek over the horizon in view, like you could reach out and grab it, it is a bit farther off than you imagined. At least for me it feels this way, hence this slow and easy transition for both Joe and me to stay in the trial world of it.

To anyone who asks, I always say that I work for Divine, Source, Father God, Spirit, or white light. I have many favourite words that I use express to people that I ended up with the most perfect job with the most loving and perfect boss. I love my work, my clients, God, the Trinity, and the concept of anything spiritual illuminating my work and life. I love waking up not knowing anything about how my day will unfold. That throughout the course of the day the possibility exists to witness the transition to the higher form of unconditional love. There could be miracles that I get to fully participate in, or the chance to be humbled watching the healing of another human, or living essence, in my daily life. I love that I am no longer in any way, shape, or form intimidated by how much in love I am with Jesus, his Mother Mary, Mary Madeline, and the power of the Trinity of the Holy

Spirit. I am no longer intimidated by how much I am in love with any, and all, of the angels that work so hard for all of us. Especially those who seek and understand them. Even those who do not understand the powers of the gifts they lavish upon us, every single moment, as they are never asleep and still work for us when we sleep.

In sharing this deep, personal experience of living life in abundance, darkness can often accompany it. A feeling of being both blessed and saddened is common. Living honestly has allowed me to experience exactly what it is that I signed up for. Part of that is sharing with you the ins and outs of the joy I agreed to and the work I signed up for. I had no idea when I said "Yes" to Source that you cannot stop working for Source, ever!! It is not in the obvious part of the contract you align your soul with, it is found written in the fine print. You are a part of a team that is entwined within you; a braided living spiritual cord that represents a living marathon of energetic relay. It just keeps on expanding and transitioning into beautiful (and sometimes pain filled) growth. You do not go through it alone though. Your spiritual team feels it with you. This generates a certain amount comfort and an unbreakable bonding strength is formed because of this. The connection between Source and human can and will sustain, feed, shelter, and comfort you; never retiring from this place of home grown, energetic, connected caring.

The sacrifices are just part of the accountability and confirmed commitment that it takes to stay in a place of humility and love. I hope that you stay with me as I allow Source to flow through me, in a rush of energy that I can feel enter my crown, flow through my arms and out the ends of my fingers. Sometimes I can hardly keep up as the spirit that loves you (and is connected to you) wants to reach out with passion, compassion, and examples that this loving energy has taught me. It continues to saturate and permeate my very body, mind, and soul. There will be times you know it is Source speaking directly to the very core of you in the context of the words, or specific chapters, and there will be times you have my version of what something has meant to me, learning and relearning a particularly hard lesson of virtue, intentions, forgiveness, and self-love. I know this to be true, no matter how old I get or how wise I become, I will in all ways love that we are gifts to be given, gifts to receive, gifts to share, and gifts to treasure. I am so blessed to know this from the deepest level of every single lesson and every single experience we are given.

WHAT IS GREY MATTER?

What is grey matter? This is a good question that deserves a good answer. In colour psychology, grey represents neutrality and balance. As we know, grey is created by mixing white and black mediums together. The intensity of this colour, living between the two primary shades of black and white, is determined by how much of each is put into the mixture. When used as a medium in the art world, it is either a colour enhancer or a toner. It can be the buffer or the breaker in the world of an artist. Grey is used on a colour palette to mix, tone or match with another colour depending on what effect you are looking for. I have read that in very olden times painters used to put their paint on slabs of marble because the grey colour of the marble did not reflect the light. Whereas, when using a white base or wooden palette, there is risk in distorting the image. Grey palettes for artists offer a toned, neutral background that allows the artist to visually see the colours as they will appear on their paintings. I have also read that the shades of grey can carry varying degrees of negative connotations. Particularly when it comes to depression or loss. The absence of colour can make things dull on many levels, tri-dimensionally speaking. I will be going back and forth between what I know grey matter to be and what it represents for me. Specifically, how living in the grey acts like a bridge in the duality of our daily life – our soul and spiritual side mixed with our logical and tangible side. I will explain the use of both methods in the practicum or practice in the human sense, as structure and the soul essence of what grey has come to represent for me. I have grown quite fond of the many shades of grey that I have become aware of, as I pay attention to them throughout my daily practice of living in the grey. Now, more than ever, living in the grey (or middle) matters to me. I will elaborate further in a future chapter more specifically what I have learned and continue to learn, so that I may share this gentle discovery with others.

If we search "What is Grey Matter?" on the internet, we get a physical description stating that the central nervous system is made up of tissue known as grey matter and white matter. Grey matter (or gray matter) makes up the outermost layer of the brain and is pinkish grey in tone. As I was researching what the literal context and meaning of grey matter was, I discovered that it is an essential component for our brains to function in a way that allows us to live fully consciously in our bodies. Grey matter is therefore vital in all aspects of life. Grey matter is formed in early development from ectoderm (the outermost layer of cells or tissue of an embryo). It continues to divide into specific cells until the entire central nervous system, both brain and spinal cord, has formed. Throughout development the volume of grey matter continues to form until the age of about 8 years old. Also, interesting to read, after this age grey matter begins to decrease in the areas of the brain but the density of the matter increases. This increase in density allows for higher processing and further mental development of humans.

Prior to now, I have not had the urge to, firstly, understand or even look up what grey matter did and secondly, what it was able to provide regarding my brain/ego development. In learning and reading about the brain, the fascination and complexity of it all gave me a better understanding of the power and substance of the matter with which I was born. It has grown along with me. Giving me all the extra tools and service, it has provided me the ability to be of both worlds. This was just the very beginning for me as our brains, bodies, and organs are so much more than I ever took the time to realize before now. Let alone appreciate and express gratitude for them, for the thankless job they often do, in keeping me in the game of walking, talking, thinking and being.

We are all complex and unique beings living consciously and unconsciously. When we are conscious, we get to cohesively decide on listening, obeying, disobeying our bodies and minds, deciding on joining in a health or unhealthy choice in the ongoing body, mind, and spirit. We are in constant communication with our beings. It always comes down to choosing!

What is the grey matter? In reading more about this topic, I have discovered that new research shows that our brains grey matter holds secrets to understand ourselves. A recent study at Harvard University showed that significant differences occur in the brains of people who meditate. This author goes on to also say "although that is good news for people who take the time to meditate, it is also good news for restless people whose minds whirl from one thought to the next, whose bodies would rather vacuum, or have a thought to take out the trash, rather on deciding and choosing to sit calmly in meditation or lie down and say Ohm." The author's argument between Ego and Spirit is "How can I gain steps on my Fitbit exercise tracker if I'm sitting down or, lying in bed meditating?"

This author suggests the Harvard study represents a wake-up call to those of us who refuse to settle down to a nice 20-minute relaxation session each morning before work, or at night before bed. This is especially useful information so I would like to write a bit more detail in the findings of this study. Neuroscientists found that it took an overall of less than 30 minutes per day, for as few as eight short weeks, to see a measurable difference in the brains of people who took the time to practice meditation. The relaxed group enjoyed feeling well and felt more relaxed. Interesting that the people who chose meditation also showed an increased volume in their grey matter. Their grey matter was denser in the hippocampus of their brain. Ironically, the region of your brain that is responsible for compassion, learning, and introspection. Moreover, their cerebral cortexes were thicker, which results in better focus, attention, and emotional integration. The study turns out evidence as it discovers meditators, even amateur meditators, have an advantage in emotional indigence. I want to leave this chapter with this thought. The more grey matter you have in your decision making and thought processing part of your brain, the better your ability to evaluate rewards and consequences! Thank you, Pamela Milam from Spirituality & Health Magazine.

HOW DOES ONE BEFRIEND GREY MATTER?

How do we begin to befriend grey energy? This is the question that has lingered on me the past forty-eight hours. This overwhelming darkness that has been lining my stomach and causing some sleepless nights; actively invading my subconscious state of peaceful rest. It is that old nagging sense of "Who do you think you are? What are you trying to prove? How are you going to deliver all that you promise?" It is a struggle battling the dark and light within me. The shadows that appear when you do something decent and good, from a place of honesty, in the work or the light to which you have committed. Where does it come from? What effect does it have on you?

I will speak in the only way I know how, to try and answer these questions. I will share with you how this energy affects me and my ability to maneuver in, around and through the congestion of all this substance. Let me start with the first question, "How do we become friends with the grey matter?" the floating balance between darkness and light. For me, the answer is choosing to become friends with the grey matter. It took me a long time to arrive at this answer though. In reflection, of all the experiences I have had over the first half of my life, I needed to get to a place where I could understand the choices, the experiences, and the outcome. In that time, I was learning about pain, suffering, selfishness, brokenness, heartaches, the short and long end of the stick, the repercussions, and the outcome of choice. I also know and understand this deeply, as I would not have any material from which to choose other endings, or options, had I not had the experiences I received. All the exposure to my circumstances growing up were all lessons I agreed to go through. Although at the time some outcomes of situations did not seem fair collectively, I understand that my soul has allowed me to accept the choices and the path that lead me here. So, in this blessing of being able to come out the other side of darkness, the loneliness related to the dark blanket that kept me, it is in the releasing of the lesson and wanting to befriend the middle that allowed me a way to reconnect with my birthright of free loving, free flowing and unconditional love. This awareness and the connected experience in the releasing and the acceptance of my past behaviour allowed me to befriend the middle of both worlds. Befriending the grey and allowing that flexibility, as I am the common denominator.

"What are you trying to prove?" Good question, right? I have asked myself this question repeatedly for many years. What I have come up with is, to just stop trying to prove anything. I tell myself to be accountable in thoughts, prayers, agendas, intentions and stop trying so hard to make a difference! Stop trying to be heard in an area of competing voices that gets louder and louder. Every single day the world becomes less and less about the goodness and the light. I remind myself to be Tracey; just be the love you come from, the honour that you know you are, working in a place that has no room for any conditional voices or a place where you need to shout your truth from the mountain top. Tracey, get out of your own way and love the holes and the cracks in the most broken of people; if they allow your essence in, just be. Do not spend any more time trying to stand out in an arena that has no room for light. In a place and space where people just want to feel their worthiness, make room for them to shine in the pin prick of light you are shinning for them. If they can feel this light, this essence, this love from the light you offer by rising above what you need to prove, then they may see they do not have a need to prove either. Be that example of loving light so it's not a threat to their extinction, or the erasing of their eternal essence. This light is a lifeline of love in a nonthreatening gesture of understanding the soul connection we are all part of.

"How are we going to deliver what we promise?" This is an incredibly good question. Just how we are supposed to deliver everything we promise? Most of us have common thread denominators. We all can get caught up in people pleasing, giving the best of ourselves to someone we know well and love. Alternatively, most of us also know which buttons to press to momentarily hurt or break the spirit of a person we love, to the core of their heart, on any given day. We all have the power within us to build up and put someone on a pedestal because of love or destroy the very same person by uttering sentences of toxic words born out of negative emotions. We all have very distinct memories of how both scenarios can play out. I will give you two of mine so you can see where I am going with this.

Breaking a heart is never my intention and it was especially true on one specific day, over twenty-five years ago. I witnessed the breaking of her heart. I felt it and I still can feel the residual effect and the outcome for her. I chose to talk about this now because she was the victim of a vicious attack that changed her heart and mine. This woman is no longer living with us in this realm, but I am sure she soars everywhere in spirit. She was gentle, kind, wise, sweet, a good listener, considerate and proper. Being of British heritage she honed her diplomacy skills and had an easy way of avoiding any confrontational or controversial situation. Often choosing to take the higher road, knowing that she was smart to do so. Her working for many years in Human Resources undoubtedly taught her the art of balancing in the middle, what I deem as the grey matter, on a regular basis. She trusted me, I trusted her, she was always an advocate, and she was kind despite my ignorance.

There was one specific day at work that I recall witnessing another employee bully this woman. This employee was very well known for her role in administering the harsher ways of communication. She brought out her "best" on my friend in this moment and lessons destroyed this woman in front of my very eyes. Tearing her apart piece by piece leaving only her shocked, white face and submissive posture in her fury. Her lifeless eyes searching the room until they rested upon where I and another woman were seated. We both bore witness to this attack. She wordlessly looked around for a lifeline, someone to defend her or offer a shred of love. The other women and I sat in shock. In our shock at what had just transpired, we allowed this to happen. We allowed ourselves to be swallowed by the wet, coldness of dark energy that continued to eat the flesh off this victim of attack and we did nothing.

I remember walking to the bathroom shaking in shock. I remember the gentle closing of the victim's office door after the assault. I remember the feeling of the closing and the locking of her broken heart. Things were never ever the same in our community of close-knit co-workers. As a result of that incident, the small team disbanded and we all became puppets to the isolation that continued to break hearts.

I cannot undo my ignorance regarding that situation and to this day still haunts me to my core. What I can do is forgive myself for the lack of consideration, support and kindness I could have shown to this woman who was being so bullied, bruised and abused. I could have stood by her side. I could have chosen to be less of a coward and more of an ambassador of love and peace. I could have defended this woman even if it were just to stand silently beside her and support her in action. I chose to do nothing and in the nothing, she never returned from the brokenness her heart suffered that day.

What that experience taught me is to use my voice, if I am ever a witness to that type of situation again, as a way of honouring my friend. As she did not deserve what happened to her that day.

The second memory I would like to share with you will illustrate the other side of grey, the while light side, and the effect you can have on a total stranger if you stay true to the light. That means looking past the human emotions of what someone might think or say. When you see the light of God in another, you must stop in mid action and recognize when spirit is calling you to the deeper meaning and action of unconditional love. It was wintertime and cold out. During this time, I was living in a little condominium. I was happy, free, and finding ways to discover who I was and what I was supposed to experience next. I made a trek to the No Frills grocery store. I was on my way in and had my coat hood buried around my face when a middle-aged man stopped me. He grabbed my arm in a way that suggested he was wanting to get my attention; not aggressive, but desperate. I stopped dead in my tracks, looked in to his sad, pleading eyes and listened to him tell his tale. He was out of work; he was waiting for his month end funds to come in; his wife was at home taking care of two small children as they could not afford the day care. He went on to tell me they had an unforeseen expense with their hydro bill, and they were trying to catch up on it. He needed to buy some food for his family for dinner. I felt all kinds of things squirming around in my head for him and myself. One of those being doubt about the story he told, which I am ashamed to admit. Also sorrow for this man who was struggling, trying to help his family.

I did give him some money and proceeded to follow him secretly and discretely into the store. I watched him from a distance buy some ground beef, a loaf of bread, margarine, eggs, cans of vegetables, potatoes, and milk. Watching him purchase these items I realized that this man was telling me his truth. I could not stop the tears that were flowing, embarrassing me from a very deep place in the middle of me. Thinking how proud I was that he asked me and how proud I was of him taking care of business for his family. His having enough guts to ask a stranger for something they desperately needed. This act of love he showed for his two children at home etched on my heart that day and will forever remain. You know the candy bin at the beginning of the checkout, where they put chocolate bars on sale sometimes if they are close to expiration date? He stopped, looked at the bin and picked up two chocolate bars, thought about it for a second and put them back. Then with a smile of love, the magnitude of which I cannot even begin to tell you, spread across this face, thinking about how this would be a nice treat for his children. He scooped up the chocolate bars and purchased them with the other items. I went back to my car, turned on the heater and sat in comfort and silence crying like a baby for at least fifteen minutes. Taking the gift in, receiving the white light of it, and the warmth of that interaction of unconditional love.

The difference between these lessons for me is not the black, and not the white, but the grey balancing both in a full understanding of what their personal experience offered. Thus, allowing full acceptance of the lesson no matter where it comes from, framing your choices and your experience in the lessons. Seeking answers in the outcome and always choosing to rise above the lessons to learn the messages they hold inside. Living in the grey matters!!!

WHY I CHOOSE TO LIVE IN THE GREY

For me, it is simple. To look at each situation from only one angle no longer serves a purpose for me. I no longer view, or define, any circumstance as "black and white." Hence, I live more in the grey which allows me to be more open-minded and objective to both sides of the situation. Living in the grey matter creates an environment that is more sedated and open, instead of being drawn to either side and having a polarized opinion about the incident, or issue. I have witnessed the power struggle between dark and light. Dark energy constantly collides with an unwavering, unmoving, wall of white light love. It remains conflicted in a battle it can never win. This division of each side, and their established boundaries, creates the foundation for me to understand the experience personally, so I can share what I have learned. Looking at each irritation, or conflict, that arises creates an opportunity to practice living in the grey and serves as evidence that the decision to do so has made a profoundly positive impact to my life. Living in the grey does not mean that I am not vulnerable or tempted by the darkness, I just have more experience managing it. When these moments occur, I am aware enough to pause and recognize the darkness, but instead of succumbing to it, I acknowledge its presence, power, and thank it for teaching me what it needs to in the moment, and then fully reject it. Dark energy lives, feeds, and breeds off energy that comes from fear related anxiety that has been given permission, from you its host, to control and manipulate you. Knowing this is half the battle. So, I do not fear it but choose to address the ignorance for what it is, stating this directly about the source of the dark energy, either verbally or with my inner voice. I do not need, or wish, to engage with it any longer than necessary. Dark energy tries to gain control by preying on and feeding our egos. This energy quickly understands I am not available and moves on to another power source. It is always looking for the path of least resistance, where it does not have to exert much energy to feed its motive. Darkness is something we all face in one way or another, for as long as we live here on this planet. As I have chosen to stay living in the grey, it matters more than ever to be wise in the existence of it. The education I have received from these dark lessons has provided me with an advantage. Knowing my enemy and its strategy well, it leaves no room for guessing where it is going, what it is up to and how it wants to control my vessel. It also has given me the complete understanding of how to fight it off and know what I need to do to; stay as calm as possible in all their storms, as they are always headed toward destruction.

Living in the grey allows me to align with its energy, combined with mine. This white light army of unconditional, nonjudgmental love aligns my energy to match the ambassadors the energy sends my way. These spirit guided beings of love never interfere unless asked upon for tools, messages, or guidance. They watch over us and protect us, and remain as so, unless they are asked upon, by us. They are often holding space for us and are witnesses to our lessons. I have witnessed far too many divine interventions to pretend they do not happen. These miracles of shifting, lifting, and shedding are a true gift to see but are never mine to share. They happen when the person is asking for this gift; the shedding and releasing of unwanted toxins or scar tissue. As light workers, we are blessed to be a witness to them, when they occur.

The white light energy is so organically natural in the shedding of light that, if invited, becomes attractive and infectious in the way that it allows you to feel internally and externally lighter, brighter, and happier. This light white energy has a way of softening the receiving of it. It is not harsh, nor does it deplete anything from you. It is the agent of healing and whole love in an energy that can encompass your very being. If you allow it to work its magic it can also help your elevation to another state of peace which, for me, creates an insurmountable fountain of joy. If you are carrying heavy burdens, this light is there waiting and inviting you to release the burden right into its unconditional, unending presence. Think about this for just a moment. This energy is grander, larger, and brighter than anything you could mentally or physically fathom, yet this energy is willing and able to meet you where you are comfortable receiving it. It is a constant and is the most consistent love you have ever tried to imagine, and it sustains you in the way that this love accepts you in every state, form, choice, and reaction you make. This energy never, ever judges you, but instead is fully accepting of all the things you need to discover, uncover, and lessons you need to learn, or even deeper, the ones you decide to not learn. How absolutely freeing to know that we are all privy to these expressions and experiences if we are open to receiving them.

Living in the grey gives you perspective, support, and mindfulness of providing answers without emotional responses. You might want to argue this but just hear me out. When I stay in the middle, or my "grey space" that I refer to it as, I remain neutral. (My friend calls her neutral spot "the grey rock," which I love and wanted to share). Dark energy comes every day to teach me things that can crush me, own me, or captivate me. At times, I have noticed a sense of paralysis, like I am not even breathing. In these moments, the pain is so raw, because of the lesson within it. I stay in the grey by blocking the attack of energy wanting to lure me into a place where it can feed off my body and soul. In the moment the darkness has revealed itself, I ask myself what I need to accept and take ownership of. Acknowledging these quickly, releases the grip of the darkness and promotes a shift in the situation. The battle is distinguished by the white light army surrounding the situation in spirit. You disengage from the darkness as an ambassador of love and truth and the battle does not have fuel to sustain the fight.

I will get personal here to explain this further. What I am about to share is still very fresh, but it was very real. I was put in the middle of a very touchy situation recently, and it was complicated. Most huge battles of the will are, but this one was personal and, of course, my ego jumped at a chance to bring two people together, on common ground. As the lesson unfolded my ego got lost in a place of disrespect. I created a very deep wound for someone I love. The lesson continued to reveal the deeper meaning. When the situation occurred, I did not give a second thought to the disrespect I had shown to a person's personal, or workspace boundaries. I walked into it with an "on my high horse" mentality, acting like I had all the answers to an extremely complicated battle. I was put in my place with a huge slap to my ego, bruise to my heart and absolute pain of deep regret. I for the first time listened to an ongoing message that I had not been adhering to. Here is the biggest part of this lesson. I had a live Thursday Namaste video scheduled in the next hour. My heart was crushed, and I was still in shock, but I make a promise weekly to show up. This video was intense and very raw. I always speak from personal experience, and while it was still intensely emotional, and I had not yet fully digested the situation, somehow, I managed to get through the talk. I was vulnerable and shared with my audience my raw state of real-life truth. I talked about it and then we talked about how to sprinkle the magic on tricky situations. I was able to recover by choosing the middle ground, the grey rock, the life support of connection to other light workers and with the viewers that show up looking for the light. I was able to work through this brokenness and find the light in the others that hold space for all of us.

After the live session, I took the time to sit with my part of the pain filled exchange and the pain I had caused. For the next few hours, I sifted through what had transpired. Eventually I apologized, sincerely, for my behaviour and my over emotional ego. The perspective given to me yesterday, was that I had to edge God out of this situation. I was reacting and acting as if I was working for Source. When I took my timeout, I realized that I needed to sidestep Him for this, to find the clarity that was required to move forward. It allowed me to feel, experience, accept and forgive the truth of the situation, for myself and in others involved. I understood, beyond anything, that the respect I have for my husband at his work is a different kind of respect I have for him in our home. I came to the middle of that truth yesterday and it felt good. I know I will never ever again disrespect that space the same way I thought I owned it beforehand. Hugely humbling. He respects me for me and allows me to be, blossom, guide, and facilitate in my work and never, ever interrupts the flow of my work with a personal need of his own. I felt huge heart pain when I realized I do not represent the same respect in my actions for him. I also learned I need to be personally accountable at giving more time and effort, so that I do not first react emotionally. Now, I take time and I give the quiet respect and space deserved before action is taken.

Back to why it is so imperative to live in the grey matter. The quiet space matters more than anything else you could ever do for your spiritual wellbeing, for the rest of your entire life. This matters because it defuses battles, wars, and emotional imbalance. It aligns the truth and sets you free from holding all the heavy density that belongs to an energy that sustains its life by feeding your egos huge desire to be heard, resulting in your thinking that you alone have all the answers to every situation that you are involved in. Thinking that you and you alone have the golden key of unlocking pain, greed, lust, power. Ask yourself, do you really want to be manipulated and possessed by this dark, energetic, subliminal, spiritual slavery? Or do you want to take a sidestep out of it? Defusing the power, by pulling the cord and sliding into the middle of your world, in the grey where you can breathe, take a moment to choose your weapon and then use that tool to cut the darkness. What this does for you is it is allowing an opening to that white, unconditional loving, ever present, sweet, soft, energy to shine in and through and around you. By doing so you are cleaning the darkness, the heaviness, and the ugliness away. When you live in the grey you clearly see, feel, and know the gift of all sides and all ways. You get to choose the grey grace of your lessons.

I will conclude this chapter with the thoughts of another light worker, her name is Sarah. Sweet Sarah, who after reading the premise of this unedited chapter had these words. "I had to listen a couple of times because there are little treasures in many sections in this chapter to consider. I needed to take some time for thought and reflection. I never utterly understood what you meant by the grey area. Now I get it and it makes perfect sense. The key is to try and stay in the grey. In the staying there I can see the other two energies, black/white clearly in the roles they chose to be dedicated to. I bear witness to the way they co-mingle as they will, and then I decipher, take what I need, absorb, and re-integrate the information that sits best within me." Sarah really got what the message is. She was able to stay calm and secure in the middle of her world, in a place where she was not threatened by holding onto fear. This view provided the clarity needed to not engage in the battle, it allowed her to witness it, without the emotional affects. She was able to watch the battle of the darkness trying to overtake the light. Sarah could see and feel that the choice was hers to experience from a perspective of sheer clarity. This clarity allowed the lesson to stay in the core of her being, giving birth to a forged tool she can use in any way she chooses to wield it. In conclusion, the lesson was worth taking a step out of her comfort zone and bearing witness. Her gift in doing so was receiving the tool she has recently secured, adding it to all the other tools she has earned.

WHY WOULD YOU CHOOSE TO LIVE IN THE GREY?

This is a particularly good question to ask yourself. I have contemplated this question many times since first hearing God's voice whisper to me in the shower, the title of this latest book. I have been asking Source what messages I am to relay in the experiences I am living in these times. To say we have been personally and worldly challenged to the degree we all have been, over the last couple of years, is an understatement. We have been challenged to survive and find a solution. I challenge everyone who is reading this to find that solution internally first and bring it out and share what your findings are with the problems you are facing in your external world. How does one do this? First, by saying "yes" and taking a deep dive into your cosmic connections. Secondly, ask for assistance. This assistance can only be taught, directed, and shown to you by faith, trust, and communication with something that is not a visual, physical substance. Connecting with something other than yourself in this cosmic way allows the other unseen energies to work and collaborate with you. This is your first commitment to self and finding your way to the middle, or centre, that I call the grey matter.

I wanted to share with you a cool gift I received a few years ago. I stated previously that for me my signs are usually delivered to me in my dreams. Sometimes they are noticeably clear and precise and other times they are not clear at all and it can take a few days for the dreams to make sense to me. This dream I am about to share with you was clear. To this day, I share the gifts as tools for many of my clients looking for clarity and a way to advance in the obstacles that they accumulate in their heart space. Sometimes we hold on to pain and lessons as weapons, so we can retain a sense of feeling safe, that justifies why we are not forgiving or releasing. Sometimes we hold on to this trauma because we know what it feels like to be a victim and this pain allows us the right to hold on to it, reminding us that we have the power to hurt back. I just know for me it was not healthy to hold on to anything that did not, and will not, serve me in my service of love and light.

I recall before I went to sleep that night, I asked for Jesus to send me something to give the people in the Healing Circle that I had been facilitating for Source for quite a while. The Healing Circle was a sacred space, a place where attendees ranged from a group of fifteen to thirty people who gathered once a month to share, heal, and grow. This Circle was space we all felt safe in. We would open the Circle by passing a healing stick around the group and whoever had the stick, had the floor. Some people never did share, and others shared a lot. I remember this one person, for months she passed the stick with a smile that lit up the room. She never spoke with her words, but she had many things to say in her presence. She was precious. I still feel her, and her energy and it has been several years (due to Covid) that we have not been able to be together.

In the dream, I was with a client and it felt so real that I know it was happening but, in another world, the spiritual world. Jesus was beside me. He was kind, loving, warm and gentle, like it was normal for Him to be standing by my side! I could feel his smile, as if to say "Yes, honey I am here, and it is normal. Just relax because I have gifts for everyone because you have asked for them." I just accepted this and continued to work in my dream, asking the client (who was on my table in my workroom) to choose a colour. He chose a violet shade of purple. I heard Jesus say, "Ok, tell this client that the colour that he chooses will be leaving his body with his DNA and he will not be affected by the leaving and we will bring it all back shortly." I reiterated to my client what was happening and my client agreed. The moment he did I saw pieces of his body, in the symbols of his DNA mixed with the violet colour, leave his body into the hands of Jesus.

I was witness then to a room beyond my room that was suspended in the universe, an acrylic box, about the size of a living room space. The floor, walls and the ceiling were all clear. There was a long, steel looking table in the middle of the space that looked heavy and light at the same time. It was secured in place to the clear acrylic floor. It was at this time I could see another being in the room, he looked human and was standing at the right-hand side of the table. He seemed very intent on receiving this material from Jesus, which had the client's symbols and colour embedded together. The manly being was tall and thin; he had a long white lab coat on, wiry hair and small glasses on the bridge of his nose. He did not even register I was witnessing his work. Then the material went through his hands and came out the other side; the material and the DNA resembled medieval chain link armour. This is the best way I can describe it to you. It was piled high on the steel table on which he was working.

At the other end of the table were three spiritual beings. I was told that they were the trinity of divine spirit here to work as well. This was the first time I heard the words Heart Filter System. This is what they were presenting me; this was the gift they were offering for anyone seeking this clarity. At the front of the table Jesus stood with his back to me with his arms spread out, as if to put a circle of love around this work.

That was all I was and am ever privy to, any time this gift is offered to a person, a client, or a group. The rest of their work is not my business and is between the gifting and the receiving of this gift. That is until Jesus taps me on the shoulder, and I am to receive it and then I have another job to do, which I elaborate on in a few minutes. However, I would like to tell you what this gift has done for me on a personal level as that night, when delivering this gift at the Circle for Source, I also received my very own Heart Filter System.

As I mentioned, it started with the tap I received on my shoulder in the dream. A gentle tap to get my attention and then I turn and feel the presence of Jesus. I see a manly figure standing in front of me, holding out his arms, with a small, velvet lined vessel. I want to say it is more like a container and it is also acrylic, so I can see the colour of the filter; it looks like knitted medieval chain link armor like the mesh that a soldier would have worn under their battle armour. I feel, more than I can see, the smile on Jesus's face as the light behind him from Spirit is too bright for me to clearly see his facial features; feeling his smile spread into my being. He hands me the precious heart filter and I am instructed to breathe it into my lungs, holding my breath long enough to exhale it back into the client receiving the gift. Before I do this, I take a moment to thank Jesus and his team for creating and bestowing this gift on me and on behalf of the client. I also thanked Jesus for allowing me to facilitate the receiving of it.

This gift is now what I commonly refer to as my violet breath. First, I blow the filter around the heart of the receiver. It wraps around their heart like a hard candy apple wrapper would wrap itself around the apple. I then blow a breath into the third eye of the receiver, linking the breath to the temple. Finally, I exhale another little violet breath to seal the filter in place.

The night I received my heart filter, which was at least five years ago, I can still hear the voice of Jesus saying, "Tracey, you do not get to pick your colour." I was extremely disappointed as I was envisioning hues of aqua and violets and orange sunsets. My message was, "Your colour is battleship grey!" Yes, grey and it was not even a nice shade of grey, it was battleship grey. Of course, I was as surprised as you are, all these years later drafting a book called *Living in the Grey Matters*! But I do not question Spirit. I did not then, and I do not now, because Spirit always knows exactly what I need and why I need it.

That night years ago we were all gifted a treasure, a tool, a visual that has many times allowed me to move on and let go of what belongs to me and what does not belong.

Over time, this heart filter system has developed and morphed into one of my best tools. This tool has provided clarity and hands on experience of what is personal for me. During a connection of communication, or even an altercation with another, that could be the most aggressive personal form of attacking, and energetically trying to claim my power, I am able to not take it personally. It is not that I am not affected by the assault because I am human and it does affect, hurt, and sometimes cripple me. I have extra ammunition now. I have a grace filled maturity due to the practice of being in enough peace to release what does not belong to me. This releasing allows me to shake off the pain and realign with the heart filter that is obviously doing its job. The moment I received this gift it reminded me of the Timex watch slogan, "Life is ticking. It takes a lickin,' but it keeps on tickin.' The heart filter is just like that, it keeps on working, reminding me that I can filter through and sort out what are my lessons in every interaction I have, in every moment I get to experience them.

The bonus in receiving this gift from Jesus is that you do not have to keep what is not yours to keep. Do not allow it to linger, hold on to it, or dissect it. You just get to let it come in, keep what is yours to work on and forgive yourself, as well as forgive the person who is dumping their hurt on you. This is an important part of the freedom you will receive and then gently let the rest go as it is runs through this finely, blessed, divine filter.

I guess at this point you might ask me a few questions. What in the heck does this have to do with the title of this chapter? Why would you choose to live in the grey? What does this gift have to do with being in the middle of the balance? The grey, loving equilibrium meeting in the middle of your heart seems to provide a way to sustain our balance, our focus, our direction daily. I challenge you here and boldly ask, why wouldn't you? If you could have access to these tools, the only cost to you is time and personal investment to whole self-health. As Dr. Dyer wrote, "Change your thoughts - Change your life!" Why would not you want to invest in the best investment you could ever make in your entire life, YOU! Be open to exploring the possibility of a personal miracle. The kind that, in its sacredness, shifts something so profoundly personal for you, there are no words to equate or state even what the shift is allowing you to experience.

I share all my gifts I receive from Source, repeatedly, to anyone who needs to have the experience. I believe it has permitted me to grow in a way that has allowed me and my ego to explore once again something so personal that it was life changing in the smallest, sweetest, and biggest way possible. Like the song "I Believe in Miracles," I have witnessed a soul being set free. I am talking about my very own soul. I am referring to the time, energy and love it takes to dedicate everything to the purpose of teaching and directing others in this way of life. I will do this by using my own examples, my own continued sharing of gifts and distributing them to anyone seeking something this beautiful. Why would you choose to live in the grey? The grey allows you to view situations from every angle. The grey will teach you all the things you need to learn so you can balance the tight rope of life. This means not just saying you will live in the grey, it means "walking the walk." Your being becomes equal with your talk of living in the grey by creating more authentic behaviours. This in turns is what manifests your future in light with love.

LIVING IN THE GREY BETWEEN COUNTRIES

Recently I was able to experience a stepping out of the norm by living on another continent for three months. The difference being that this was not entirely vacation time for us. Working fulltime, many of us allow ourselves the traditional one, two, or even three weeks of regulated, earned, or acquired vacation time. We all feel we have earned time away from the hustle and bustle of work, home, schedules, mandates, responsibilities that build character, and structure, in our life. Our ability to be able to spend this time away was earned and planned for, not unlike others at our age and stage of life. Some people are just lucky to live this way, in freedom of choice, most of their life. The time away for, if it was granted to Joe and me this year, was the gift of living and working in a new home space. People kept referring to our time away as vacation and I can understand the thoughts behind our time away. We are close to retiring, or more accurately, semi retiring and yet we worked just as hard in our jobs and careers in Mexico, as much as we did in Canada.

Yes, we had escaped the cold and winter months in Canada, but our time away was not considered a traditional vacation, a place without work. It was more akin to a location change for the two of us. I thought we had made it truly clear we were still working, and we were available for anything anyone needed. It was an adjustment mentally, a slowing down both in our minds and in our bodies. We were able to hear the silence when we allowed ourselves to listen. Waking, every day to the warmth of the sun, blue sky and the mountains surrounding us in a vastness of space, expanding our hearts to receive it, while quietly drinking our delicious coffee. It was real and surreal at the same time. It inspired us to be our best selves when engaged in work and when quietly sitting in the same space, absorbing all the gifts we were receiving.

This experience was a brand-new chapter of living in a new location. A test, a quest to see what we could discover in the new space, both in ourselves and in each other. Joe and I are quite spontaneous when it comes to adventure, so we did a lot of "firsts" in Tequisquiapan. We bought a motorcycle and tacked on three thousand kilometers before we tucked it away in storage. We traveled and explored the town we live in and the small towns around us. We took our laundry to a little place we found in the area, which did an excellent job. We bought a printer; I carried it home, tucked firmly behind Joe on the bike from San Juan - forty minutes away. All the while looking like the locals, who manage to carry everything on their bikes it seems. One time we passed a family of four on the back a single motorcycle! It was all learning and adapting to our new home away from home.

Throughout our duration I never, ever felt like I did not belong, fit in or was looked down upon by any of the locals that live, thrive, and work in this town. I felt welcomed from a place and space deep inside the hearts and souls of these local people. Joe and I quickly slipped into our routine. Routine is so bound within us. The implementation of routine is no longer a mystery to me, why it is that human beings can find it hard to allow the slower pace of retirement to creep in. It is more of an acceptance to something, a sense of order. We are two people who work well with structure and planning, and I think, simultaneously, we both felt a little bit of guilt for operating this way in Mexico. We soon understood, over the course of those three months, that we did not have to hold on to it and started to let it go; bit by bit, slowly shedding it in the soil that surrounded us. Our routine consisted of early morning rising. Sometimes for me as early as 6:30am, especially if I had an early morning virtual session. Otherwise, I started most mornings around 7:00am and worked until around 1:00pm daily.

Joe would get the coffee going and would quietly bring me one to my workstation. Joe found his own rhythm and worked those mornings as well; it was quietly perfect as we found a way to be who we needed to be and be mindful of each other's work. This took about a month to fall into place, and we still had workers coming and going finishing construction in our new place. Being present in our space that was not fully completed yet allowed us a voice in the things we needed adjusted or added to our new space. We would have breakfast together most days, in between work, and would meet up again for lunch, where we would make plans for the rest of our day. Some days we did not do anything productive physically but so much was developing inside of us, stepping out of old routines, and creating new ones. Some days I felt restless, and on those days, I ventured out to spend time walking, shopping, praying, or meditating. Joe also realized there were things he needed to let go of; things that were changing in the experience he was living in. I also allowed myself time to grow. I felt terrible when I found out people were texting me and trying to call me leaving messages I could not retrieve. I had not even thought about those clients, connections that did not know I had exchanged my Canadian phone chip for a less expensive phone chip while we were out of the country. I was able to access my emails and my Facebook messenger but not my Canadian cell phone number. That too was something I needed to find accountability in and claim responsibility for. Learning curves never, ever go away. They just keep reappearing so we can gain the knowledge we need to learn in the acceptance, then the forgiveness required and of course the releasing of it.

In this time away I was able to let go of the lessons that continued to trigger me. I learned to hold space for people with whom I do not always agree. Those who, in their passion have their own powerful thoughts about what is right or wrong, true, or not true for themselves, as well as their right of expressing this to others. What I gathered is that we all have a voice and we all have an opinion and a right to express it. I reached deep inside of myself when I was faced with an irritation, judgment, or comment I received and had a tough time digesting it. I stopped defending myself when delivering the truth, as I saw it, instead of expressing it in a way of opposition filled with emotion. I accepted the lesson, sometimes feeling it in the pit of my solar plexus and sometimes directed to the middle of my heart. I stopped worrying about how someone might take what I had said, in a recorded session, and let it go straight to where it was intended. Sending it off with love and light and peace and grace. I stopped allowing myself to feel like I owed everyone all the little pieces of myself as a lifeline; giving permission to take that piece of me mostly because I did not feel worthy to stand my ground in the truth. I have been discovering the missing pieces within myself. This time away allowed me to disconnect in such a powerful way, giving me a quiet chance to discover what was left inside of me to work on, rediscover, uncover, and align. This discovery allowed me the time to be the in the grey, literally "just be." Saturated in tools, the work, the words, the cause, and effect, in all this massive shifting growth, I was able to just be.

Did I work hard? Yes. Did I play hard? Absolutely. Did I find the balance for the first time in my life? I did. What does this allow me to offer the world around me? I want to talk about what I was feeling between the two continents and how I fit in both places. Although I am human and am triggered every day by something repeating, offending, or teaching me something I need to relearn or realign, I still managed to discover my own middle ground. I find that when I am relearning something it is much more aggravating and annoying then to just accept the lesson and realign. Meaning, if I chose to realign, I spend less time in the aggravation, the interaction causing, or the irritation in the acceptance of the lesson. I also am witness now, to what I call, the snowball effect. There are times I am caught off guard and do not think through my reaction. This can cause the snowball effect that hits you and has several stages releasing the lesson. Most people when in trouble or in a situation they do not know how to address or find truth in, look for people they can use as an advantage. This gives the intended agenda a source of resource and an army

LIVING IN THE GREY MATTER

to back them up. We can and do, get caught in the crossfires of these storms. We need to be as honest as possible and release this sabotaging. This time out, this quiet space allowed me to take that time out. Allowing me the true essence of the meaning of the lesson through the intended action. What holding space does is it allows you time to stop and think about the frustration, irritation, or annoyance in a new way. It might not be the answer you are looking for, but when you can recognize it for what it is, there is grace in accepting that.

Living in North America, specifically Canada, most of my life has been a huge educational journey. I have learned the power of privacy, the power of integrity, the power of the legal system. I have learned that education is power, and in turn provides opportunity for equity, equality, and success. I am choosing to continue to grow independently but I am dependent on others as well. I have known for a long time that most Canadians are friendly, but very quietly and confidently reserved in a personal way, which is not witnessed in large crowds; most of them keeping emotionally to themselves. My experience of being Canadian is one of being kind and having huge personal boundaries of privacy. We are friendly, but lonely. Our country is one where most of us experience a life where all our basic needs are met. Some of us have far more than they will ever need in a lifetime, which can leave room for greed, or for some, the fear of losing all that they have and as a result, can feel the need to own/ hoard more than is necessary for survival. This is the energy and the awareness I have coming back to Canada, after being in the mountains for three months. This is a general observation and I will elaborate a bit more in what I feel and see around me. My neighbours on our street in Canada are pleasant. They say hello but choose to stay behind closed doors most of the time. Not just because it is wintertime, it's all year long. I meet these same people I have been sharing a street with for several years, in the grocery store or walking down the street, and they are strangers to me. They have been and will continue to be. What did I bring back from Mexico? I brought back a smile, a genuine "Hello, good to see you again" and acceptance of their privacy. Instead of feeling distant or annoyed that there is so much uncaring energy exchanged between us, I brought back love, and kindness, an open heart, mind, and time, if ever they choose to spend any of it with me. I brought back the awareness that I can bring some sunshine back home and be more aware if someone needs a kind word, or if someone needs a quiet space to stay safe in. I have learned there is no such thing as being truly safe. Meaning that we are all destined to face challenges in our life. But I need to be more considerate for the people still seeking that kind of safety, while still feeling fear. This is kindness; this is me bringing back what comes so naturally from the people I had just spent the last several months with. Most of them live their lives in poverty and challenging work. Poverty can become your biggest gift. For even with little, they share a smile and their kindness, which costs nothing but is worth everything.

What can I bring back to Mexico? I can dedicate myself to learning their language, speaking to them in their words, and trying to communicate and better understand each other. I can learn to hold space and respect the traditions that hold so much depth and faith to this residence. I can support the merchants and markets, all the locals who have their own business. I can learn that these people are proud, and I am not there to buy their love, I am there in their home and now it is my responsibility to earn that privilege. I understand deeply how hard they work, what they sacrifice, and how they live from moment to moment. Some days and they have the deepest, most reverent faith beyond words. They give everything to God; they cherish and offer many things, dedicated prayer and community prayer and leave it at the foot of the cross. This poverty does show but deeper than the poverty is the community of pride mixed with honour. It is bigger and bolder and more present than the poverty. The energy is not talked about, but it is honoured in many ways; that is beyond powerful. What I can bring to Mexico is my presence, my respect, my prayers, my faith, my work. I can and will hold space for this community and pray for them.

It is my hope that I can bring some wisdom, tools, and some sharing when, asked by the community. I will say yes, even if the yes challenges me. For example, being invited to paint a mural in support of the strength of women on a wall, in a part of the town I was not familiar with. I will say yes to bringing my faith, love, healing, and tools to anyone who asks for them. I will continue to possess an open heart, mind, and vessel, when I go back to our home in Mexico. Aware that it is a different culture, but also aware that people, no matter where they live and how they live, need unconditional acceptance and love. This has softened my perspective on something one needs to experience to understand the fullness of the richness and growth. I am going to tell you my whole truth in the closing of this chapter. I did not want to come back to Canada at the end of March. If I had my way, I would still be in Mexico happily living out the rest of my life in those mountains. I know though that I needed to come back, not only to support my life here but to bring back all the spiritual and emotionally gifts I received in this place. Continuing to be a vehicle of energy filled love and sharing it with people who need to feel this love, sharing this energy, and opening a space for acceptance. This gifting, exchanging, and education of love is a personal reminder for me that my Source, and the source of this gift, encourages me to share its grace. Share the wealth, be one with the things you struggle with the most and then release, forgive, and teach with direct action. The grace is received in the giving.

THE EYE OF THE STORM IS GREY

This chapter is near and dear to the middle ground, in the Centre of my own heart chakra. This eye of the storm has become my personal Switzerland. I have heard for many years that Switzerland stays in a state of neutral. In researching why, I use this country often to stake my claim in my healing practice of neutral. I have read other small countries take the same non-interventionist stances; Costa Rica, Ireland, and Austria, to name a few. I have read that Switzerland remains the oldest and most respected. How did it earn its most unique place in world politics? A little history lesson. I have read that the earliest move towards Swiss neutrality dated as far back as 1515 when the Swiss confederacy suffered a devastating loss to the Marignano. The article states that following the defeat, the Confederacy abandoned its expansionist policies and looked to avoid future conflict in the interest of self-preservation. It was Napoleonic Wars, however, that truly sealed Switzerland's place as a neutral nation. It is also important to note that since World War II, Switzerland has taken a more active role in international affairs by aiding with humanitarian initiatives, but Switzerland remains fiercely neutral regarding military affairs.

Why did I want to talk about this small country, the stance it holds steadfast to and for the very center of its origin? Because I personally respect this country living in the peace, unity, and the sovereign it holds dear to. The core values and people who are bound and pledged to live in this committed honouring. Living in the eye of the storm is where, for me, I get my centre, my bearings, and my information. As I read about this neutral stance that these small countries stand for in many ways, it makes me feel courage and respect for them on a level that goes deeper than the surface.

Living in the eye of the grey storm brings a certain intelligence to oneself. Something that is softer and quieter than the battle going on in our world. The noisy, congested energy of dark density that is trying desperately to gain control, resume power, and have us subliminally submit. This energy of density represented physically as a thick fog, designed for, and achieving, reduced clarity. This can be cleared away quickly by the acceptance of pure sunshine, or white light energy, into our souls. One of my favorite things to do is to sit in the quiet of darkness and just start to meditate. Holding space with the light, that simple act of faith allows me to invite the light of divinity love in. I then bear witness to the power of the light of love that continues to clear the space. Visualize the steam that dissipates off your bathroom mirror after your hot shower. It just disintegrates in front of your eyes, your mind, and your body. It, and spiritually, casts out of your surroundings and returns to where it originated. Leaving you basking in the eye, the calm, the protection in the middle of the grey, quietly sitting and observing the consistent momentum of the storm that cannot come anywhere near you. Yes, you are loved this much. Always guarded like a cherished piece of fine China, a treasure to Source. Your handpicked and designated spiritual team protects you at all costs, in every single moment you are living in this embodiment of flesh - bone, blood, organs, and spirit. At times I wish we as humans could fully understand the commitment of connection and love that divine provides us, but I also understand it may fully interfere in the soul school and worldly school lessons we are to experience and grow through to become awakened and responsible for our life purposes.

The eye of the storm, this grey haven of peace and quiet gives me personal a way to clear my whole self entirely, so that I have more clarity than ever. Understanding what I need to be, do, or co-create as a facilitator, mediator, and director of true self. This wisdom teaches me beyond anything to date that provides me timing, and amazing new tools to bring forth in any moments I am working for and working with Divine Source. This grey helps me hear the whole picture and listen deeper than I ever dreamed possible. This quiet neutral grey matter brings me the best of both worlds.

We are workers for Divine, so this might seem a bit controversial. We are not to fully align with the darker density that life challenges us with. At various points in our life, we all suffer with loss, pain and incredible, life changing lessons. How are we not supposed to act on them or defend them? I believe, with every fibre of my being, there is a huge difference between right and wrong. I have opened my mouth in a moment of passion where I know the toxic words spewing out was completely unwarranted and caused a great deal of damage and backlash. The cleanup was time consuming, energetically speaking, and some of the damage was never recovered. These horrible lessons for me are now filed away as information that is stored and accessed when I need to offer guidance to another. For example, when in a session with someone still suffering or hanging onto something that is toxic for them, I have some tools to offer, gathered from my past experiences. If they choose, I offer a helping hand to provide clarity on how to move forward. None of us should ever have to agonize or suffer through a circumstance alone. I can attest to having been present in a place of this kind of density. I have wallowed in the trenches, trying to find my way out and I was always given the gift of exiting in the most perfect, divine timing. The best way I can describe it is it felt like an ally, a gift, a presence was with me. Somehow guided by the grace of Divine who always provided the time, presence, and space needed to heal and recover.

Realizing the neutral in any situation allows you the time out during the storm, a chance to recover, a chance to discover the deeper root in the answers you seek in the confusion a storm can stir up internally. This grey peace of tranquility, you choose to step into, can give you a new sought out wisdom. This wisdom is often the glue you have been seeking to put all the broken pieces of your life back into the places it was pulled out of you. Most times, in the aftermath of a difficult situation, we hang on to the anger, the dominance, the control that others have displayed. Whatever the circumstance may be, a piece of ourselves was taken from a place we cherished, and we did not give permission for it to be taken. The emotional scars eventually heal and serve as reminders, the medals we wear if you will, from the battles we have been called into on behalf of our precious beings. Waving the white flag of forgiveness lets us breathe and recover from the pieces we have been trying to reconnect too. This is life after death in some cases. Forgiveness has many degrees and levels of cause and effect, on a body that has been on the front line of someone else's war. The glue I speak of takes a courageous heart of self-work and acknowledgment. Yes, a huge helping of forgiveness is necessary for the glue to adhere to the pieces you are trying to reattach to your internal space of the wholeness it occupied, before the attack. This grey area of compromising is your beautiful bargaining chip. This is you having a conversation with the healer within you to recognize you do not have to stay in this prison. You have served your time. You can have freedom from this and fully recover by using this information and the glue you need to rediscover a new you. This gives you the right to share with others as you together, and in conjunction with, join in the same connection of whole self. Building forces, new strength, new compassion with the same shifting love that others can relate to. This grey matter is a calling of collective intelligence that realizes the strength in communion. This creates a conscious shifting, building a healthy outlook, channeling a way to join forces in the power words that match your actions.

GREY MATTER WITH MY MOTHER

Over the past few months, every couple of days, my mom and I connect on Facebook messenger, engaging in long overdue chats and inspiring a new growth, a new understanding, between us. For the first time, in some ways, I am really hearing her in a different context. In sharing this intimate part of myself, I must confess I have not allowed time for her in this way in the past several years. This time has created space for this slow dance time between us. So, in all honesty, I am just more aware that I am present in our conversation and I am really listening, observing, and understanding her better than I ever thought possible. Here, in our little hide away from the world, I have been able to keep to and adhere to no outside pressure to be, respond, or even allow to take me over. Here, I have found a confidence to just be in the state of being. Open to hear, and respond, without the distractions that can carry us away. This has been the installment of the piece that has been missing, for both Joe and I, during our many years of service to others and self. In saying all of this it has also allowed me to be present for my momma. She rarely asks for anything. I have noticed, with the recent frequency of our conversations, that she has always wanted, no needed, to connect with me in this way, but never ever asked for what she has needed.

I have also noticed that I need to connect to her as well. The more we chat the more she reveals the things she has kept to herself over the years, and it is such a gift to know her this way. At times I wonder why it has taken her so long to share this stuff. In these conversations I see and feel her moving into the grey of her life. The sacrifices she holds dear to her along with the constant service she feels beholden to do for all of us. In the middle, where we meet, she can be her own person who has the right to talk about her feelings in this safe space. In this space she sometimes chooses to tell me things she never has before. As I listen, she heals, and when she heals, I heal and the world becomes a better place. When we both meet in the middle, not as a mother and daughter, but as two women in a deeper discussion than something as mundane as talking about the weather, or what is in the oven for dinner, or what plans are developing for the weekend. It is a beautiful place to come to know this person in this way, thereby enriching the relationship. I see, hear, and love her deeper than I ever dreamed possible.

She watches my Thursday Namaste live videos religiously and I know she tries her absolute best to follow what is being said even though she does not fully understand the messages. She understands the love, the energy, the flow and the connections. She is beyond proud but has an extremely hard way of verbally expressing with her words. She has always had a block in the throat chakra. In fact, today she said "Trace how do you talk like that? It absolutely amazes me how you open, channel, and facilitate so effortlessly, when I have a hard time stringing nine words together to form a sentence." I did my absolute best to explain that it is mostly channeled from the Divine and it flows from an educational system I work for that doesn't require much effort from me. I just say "yes" to Spirit, speak from my heart and connection of love and talk about it being my personal experience and connection with Source that brings all the words to form. For me it is all about me stepping out and Source stepping in. My mother gets the concept but does not fully understand it. She feels it deeply though, and this feeling of healing without words shifting within my mother has allowed her to explore some deep things she has kept to herself all these years. I told my mother that after a video or an intense session of full-on mediation, I do shut down and unplug sometimes for a couple of hours, not even saying one word as I allow Source to replenish me. I do take the time to unplug and realign. She was happy to hear that I do find the balance of what my body needs and what my souls needs to stay in the grey, reconnecting to whole self.

One day, I asked my mother if she had any ideas for me to talk about in a Thursday Namaste video. She surprised me with her answer and she had a lot to say. I will try to remember her words and her message today and share this with you in the next paragraph; it was immensely powerful.

I asked, "Mom any ideas for a Thursday Namaste video?" She stopped for a minute in the conversation we were having and just said to me she that she "missed her mom." I had never, ever heard my mom talk about her mom like that in a way that she was missing her. She said, "I think everyone at a certain time in their life misses their mom in one way or another." I replied, "Mom I can feel your mom wanting to hug you. Would you like me to ask Maisy to visit you and give you a big hug? I can pray for that for you." She smiled and said, "Yes, that would be nice." I said, "Well, you might truly feel her and please do not worry she is not here to hug you and bring you home to heaven yet. It is just to let you know she watches over you and is never far away from her baby." My mother loved that message and I loved telling her that message. I told her it might surprise her but to be open to her mother hugging her. That was a big moment for us both as we normally do not really talk that deeply about the spiritual side of life. That has always been tucked away, so preciously and personally in my mom's heart. After that tender moment with my mom, she finally spoke again and asked me what the age group of the people was who watched the videos. I said, "Between 28 and 85" as I wanted to include her in my answer. She then said, "Can you talk about preparing for retirement physically and emotionally?" Then she went on to say "...and preparing for death; physically, financially and emotionally." This genuinely surprised me, that she really wanted people to know, appreciate and understand the kind of planning and accountability she has felt has been lost to a younger generation.

Truly my mother melted my heart with this beautiful kindness.

She wanted the younger generation to understand that the work and effort and planning must be put in place so that a person can have the rest period they have earned throughout their life. Retirement is a time to reap what they have worked so hard in daily life to sow. The reward for the grind of being responsible for family and the life they chose to live. To share the wisdom to tuck away a bit of their hard work and efforts to save enough equity to live a life of peace and quiet. She further said she wanted this generation to understand that parents should not be responsible for what children assume they are entitled to and take for granted; hard earned integrity and savings teaches responsibility for self and others. She also stated that children should not feel they need to take care of their parents and that her generation feels very strongly about this. So, it is at this point that I feel the need to mention, it is difficult for my mother to receive money from me. She often calls me a stubborn little____ - I will let you fill in this blank. One of the most endearing things I have always loved about this passionate woman, is that we have always been able to express ourselves to each other using the most amazing combination of swear words. This has always been beyond liberating, as my mom and I love this type of release valve of expression.

She went on to further comment on the importance of planning your death. She feels it is extremely imperative to have all these details in order. In fact, my parents have all the funeral arrangements prepared, they also paid for them in advance. They have their Will finalized and all the details that go along with that; naming the Executor, the emergency contact information, where all their possessions are to be allocated and donated to – excluding a few very personal effects to their loved ones, for keepsake purposes. My father even constructed and built the boxes that their ashes will rest in, side by side. I am in awe of this kind of organization and all the planning and talks between them on a subject matter most people avoid altogether. My father and mother have their cremation paid for and set up, the cremation grave site purchased, and the black Onyx double-hearted tombstone in place; with the first part engraved with names and birthdates and two words on the top of it that melted my heart, "Together Forever."

In this conversation, I loved that she opened and wanted me to do a video on what was and still is, one of the most important things in my mother's thoughts. How she feels about how the waning of personal accountability and that external awareness has gone by the wayside in this current generation. She feels it has more noise and less respect for personal accountability than ever before. I wanted to honour my mother's legacy in a chapter in this book. I had not noticed the beautiful grey my mother wears so naturally and so passionately in her quiet reverence. Her sacredness, her own beautiful honour, and her ways of being confident, steadfast, and loyal. She is my hero on so many levels. She is the reason I have a confidence that shines through her love for me. When she hangs up, she says "I love you, my baby." I have this to carry me through when the storms come and they will. When they do, I know she will be there waiting for me in the grey of my storm in my heart space. She is a quiet legend of consistency that sustains us all in the best ways. I will drink as many drops as I can in her presence, as she fills my cup with so many gifts.

My mom has found her middle; she knows who she is, what she stands for, what she still feels so passionately about expressing. She has found a way to make the peace she evaded for the years of putting others first and the service she dedicated herself to. She has not always been in a healthy state working through her own choices or more accurately, the ones others made for her. But she chose to be steadfast. She stayed soft and pliable enough to not allow her heart to harden. She chose to rise above and quietly sort it all out. She chose love and believe me when I say, she chose unconditional love. She did the best she could with what she had to share. Living in the grey matters!!

THE HEALTHY EMPATH/UNHEALTHY EMPATH

One morning I was talking with someone that I share a lot with. We chat daily and refer to one another as each other's muse. In exchanging all that we do together, we have come to realize that each of us is a gift to, and for, the other. We have both grown so much independently, but growth also happens with the interchanging of our thoughts and ideas. Oftentimes we are sharing new insights and wisdom learned in previous conversations, after we have had time to think, process and absorb the information that was shared. Today was another one of those euphoric days of growing and sharing. It was so powerful that I really wanted to dedicate a whole chapter to this title.

I believe in mediation. Silent mediation has the power to bless the world. The world needs a lot of blessings right now. Either in solitude or a planned group session, meditation has the power to bring forth a sense of calm to the manic world around us, by quietly holding space.

We fully trust in the "Divine plan" that has been laid out in front of us, by having complete faith in the direction of the plans purpose. Humbled enough to trust, we do not need to know the outcome as it is not ours to understand. We accomplish this by trusting deeply. In this thick silence of love, we can release the victim and the perpetrator simultaneously to God source. The unraveling of the truth allows us to witness the contrast of the situation, without personal emotion. The wisdom illuminates and allows our energy to grow in the most incredible way as we witness what teamwork, in the divine world, really means. To be a part of this as a relay of love that is extended and offered in the most perfect assembly, separately, but connected, as one divine purpose. Each spiritual being with their own gifts to share.

We are all blessed when we come to realize and understand the meaning and reasons of the lessons we get to experience. This in turn allows us to hold space in the silence, without any judgment, following through with the releasing it back to God with love, from love. This cycle just keeps repeating over and over for anything and everything you are intending in your holding of this loving space. This wisdom teaches you the difference between perpetuating and polarity. This means when you meet these two powers in the middle you can choose to stay neutral. This gives equality to both powers holding space without judgment, having faith in the grander plan.

The healthy empath means you understand by seeing the complexity of the often-complicated, emotional situations you find yourself involved in. The difference is, with a healthy empath you are not picking it up personally to feel, or hold onto, someone else's pain. The healthy empath does not need to feel the pain to understand the pain. In this understanding, you can give one of the greatest gifts that every human being needs, for someone to see and understand their pain. This healthy empath is graced with the knowledge and a deep understanding of this human need. They can just show up, as they are not required to join in a lesson of absolute brokenness that does not belong to them. They simply commit to seeing, hearing, and holding a space of love for another.

This action of love allows the person in pain an opportunity to rise, versus your going down to their level and joining them in their pain. What this can teach you, and others, is by going through this process and learning the difference between healthy and unhealthy self-love, or self-sabotaging, allows you to shift and raise your vibration in the action that promotes positive productivity. The healthy empath takes an oath to protect its vessel and to rise to the occasion to bring loving energy to others.

If you choose to stay actively aware of this silent holding of space, and its perspective, you will naturally bind with other empaths. Thereby growing in numbers, connected in love.

The unhealthy empath is how I used to be. I was unhealthy for many years thinking I was doing so much good by carrying the weight of the world and layering my heart with the physical pain of others. I thought it was a huge sacrifice as well as a deep labour of love. From a small age, I was being raised and educated by the Catholic school, taught by the "sisters of the cloth." Theses sisters, who married their faith, taught us about saints and martyrs and how, in some cases, they chose to become a human sacrifice. I was always enamoured by the stories they read to us in religious studies. One story touched my soul. St. Therese, the little flower who died young, tragically sacrificing her love and life. Her love for Jesus was so beautiful that, at times, I wanted to be more like her. She was always my favorite. I read her life story and followed stories of people receiving miracles from her. For those of you reading, who are not familiar with her, let me share a bit about her. She was a Carmelite nun who lived during the late 1800s and it has been reported that she has repeatedly been the channel through which God has confirmed countless prayer intentions. It is noted that she said this before she died, "My mission – to make God loved – will begin after my death. I will spend my heaven doing good on earth. I will let fall a shower of roses." The rose novena prayer does not require a specific "formula" to invoke St. Therese's intercession. Often people will pray this for a period of nine days, and at the end of the nine days, a rose might appear to confirm that prayer intention. I would love to share with you the miracle she granted me.

When I was young, young, twenty-three, I was already married with a four-year-old and a two-year-old at home. The four of us were living in an old, yellow-brick home we managed to purchase that needed a ton of work. I remember moving into this place with a very heavy heart. The heavy heart was normal for me back then. I felt trapped, lost, misunderstood, and very broken. I had been running from myself and my brokenness for an exceptionally long time. Time stood still with so many responsibilities. Looking back now, I wished I had had a bit more patience for everything, including myself, and had allowed myself the time to mature. I am quite certain if I had tried a bit harder, and taken care of my issues, I would have been a better person. I have forgiven the person I was and am no longer. Remembering this reminds me of how it felt to be an unhealthy empath.

I remember this visit from St. Theresa like it happened just yesterday, but it was forty-one years ago this year. I was very unhappy with my husband working twelve-hour night shifts. This had been going on since our first son was born, five years prior. The shifts were long and I did not do well at night when it was dark outside. I had a lot of personal fears and deep phobias back then and struggled with, undiagnosed, postpartum depression and loneliness. I had prayed often that my husband would somehow be granted a day job in a new position, daily, to no avail. I realized this was my issue and not his, but I also thought our troubled marriage might catch a break if we were able to spend more time together forming and raising our family. I really felt lonely on so many levels I could not identify. I remember my husband coming home to share with me a new job had been posted at his work. This job was a straight day job and something that, if he were selected in the interviewing process, would require training away from home for three months. After discussing it we decided he should apply.

I then decided to recite the nine-day novena prayer, directed to St Therese, to see if she could assist with the interview. I did the prayer religiously, daily at the same time and in the same place, kneeled in the privacy of my bedroom. I prayed that my husband would have a good interview and that it would go well. I did not pray that he would get the job for I had faith that, if I asked for a valuable experience for him, the rest would just happen. In short, he did get the job, he did not have to go away to training for the three months and he started within a month of the original job posting. Here is what happened after the nine days of prayer. I was out grocery shopping, had three paper bags full of groceries and two children to tote in from the car. I started in from the van with one child on my hip, one child in front of me and one brown paper bag full of groceries. I unlocked the door, stepped into the glass porch, and opened the next door where you entered the kitchen. I was so shocked that I dropped the grocery bag on the floor and the loose oranges started to roll around on the kitchen floor. I dropped to my knees in tears. I remember Kory tugging on my sleeve saying, "Mommy are you ok?" All I could smell was the heaviest scent of red roses you could ever imagine. I put the bag down, gathering my wits and groceries, and thanked St. Therese for the sign. I continued my day getting chores done all the while knowing that things would turn out perfectly, everything aligning as it should. I had no idea that four hours later, when I walked up the stairs to the bedroom, that I would be hit in the face with another wave of roses so strong that it took the breath right out of my lungs. I sat in the middle of the staircase crying tears of joy, hope, relief, and awe. I have never had another encounter with the little flower St. Therese but wanted to share the majestic angel who came to visit me in an act of faith, on my part and pure kindness on hers.

How does this relate to the unhealthy empath? It allowed me to think past what was for me to hold on to and what is mine to share, in the healing work I have felt called to do. I used to think I had to hold all the pain in the world, like St. Therese did in her short life. That if I could not be saintly, especially after receiving a gift from a saint, that I was not doing all God was calling me to do for the greater sake of sacrifice and love. I lived many years trying to make up for all the wrong I caused and all the pain I held on to internally, thinking that holding on to it was some sort of penalty, or penance, or an act of contrition. I love that I was honored by a gift from a saint who works conjunctively with spiritual love to bring peace and gifts to others seeking it out. But it has also taught me we are all worth the experiences of real-life miracles that come in many shapes, forms, apparitions - even from the scent of a house full of roses.

The unhealthy empath lingers on the past, relying heavily on holding the weight of the world on their hearts and shoulders and equates that to their own value or self-worth. The unhealthy empath feels responsible to fix, heal, express thoughts and freely offers all the above to anyone, and everyone, that gives them the time of day. An unhealthy empath is addicted to the feeling of this and is distracted by the damage of people in pain and in need. The unhealthy empath has a huge, hungry ego that has a deep need for respect and love from others. The unhealthy empath spends a vast amount of extra time in situations that are complex and complicated so they can come out the victor in the problem solving of the situation. I know these are bold acclamations, but I am only talking about where I have been and where I no longer choose to reside.

I know firsthand that it is a process of growth to understand the differences between healthy and unhealthy empathic gifting. I know I have always been an empath. Everyone is empathic to some degree; it is part of our inheritance from spirit. It is a birth mark on your third eye. Some people know the gift and use it wisely, some people know the gift and use it unwisely. All the lessons are the prices you pay for the way you use the gifting. I will share now how I have experienced the gifts of empathic wisdom.

I noticed a year or so ago that I was laden with a heavy heart. It was extremely uncomfortable and I noticed it was getting increasingly worse. The more intense sessions in meditation to help alleviate the heaviness, the heavier the pain grew around my heart. I realized, by seeking other healing counsel, that I was holding on to the pain and the heartache of others instead of stepping out and just assisting in the releasing I was trying to hold it for them. After hearing this, I understood much more clearly that if I did not stop doing this, I would not survive the next few years. I decided to release everything and let it go. The moment I understood that the darker power of my need to feed my ego was not worth the loss of my way, or my life, I decided to release all of it and let it go.

Over the years, I have adapted to fully understanding the balance of choosing healthy empathic gifts and knowing when to step out of the way of the unhealthy habits that fed my ego and bruised my heart and space. Do I still want to, some days, be like the saint with the beautiful flowers I experienced so many long years ago? Yes, to be honest, I do feel that pull to bring a bigger meaning to everyone, to everything that matters. To experience an awakening that I have been invited to help them solve is a gift like no other. This alone is the bigger reason for me now, to continue the work of Source but stay in a more humbled state while present in someone's journey, as their process or message is shown to them. To support it by holding space for them, and to experience the love as it spreads around them, infecting their own life and their world around them. I need now, more than ever, for the healthy empathic soul of my own personal space to make it less about me and focus more on teaching what I know to others. To be a healthy empathic source versus the unhealthy empath. In realizing this, there is state of grace that presents itself. It is the best way I know how to describe the feeling and does make complete sense when you experience it for yourself.

In conclusion, understanding of the difference between the healthy empath versus the unhealthy empath is simple and not complicated at all. My own experience in this growing gift has been allowing myself to accept the slow process of the receiving of both healthy, and unhealthy, empathic, knowing wisdom. I have gathered enough knowledge to feel, see, understand, and let go of things that brought deeper pain and can release it. Thus, allowing the healthy empath to rise through the rebirth of what the unhealthy pieces of me needed to release, let go of, and give back to God. I love this part. I know that God will hold all of me; all the broken pieces that I tried to force to fit and the pieces I outgrew. These parts of me brought me a false sense of power that could not stay. If they had, I would not have been able to find the center, the balance of my middle. This healthy shift created a secure balance within me, joining all the subtle, positive, loving pieces that know fit perfectly in the space I made room for. Allowing my cognitive thinking the opportunity to work with the ever-steady, healthy, hum of my internal engine. The result is always peace-filled joy lulling you back to the centre, the middle, the grey presence of both worlds. You always get to choose where to put your energy.

HEALING IN THE GREY MATTERS

When you ask for signs and you are not specific, they show up in the strangest places. My signs, which are loud and clear, are showing up in the last hour of peace-filled, blissful sleep that awakens me. Opening my heavy eyes and sleepy head from slumber under warm covers, which want to keep me curled up in them. These signs come to me in a dreamlike, semiconscious state of being on the cusp of full consciousness. This is where I had a dream of receiving acupuncture. This is very unusual for me and because it was so unusual, it woke me up completely. I dreamt that I was being given acupuncture, receiving a miracle of healing, with so much clarity and feeling that it shocked me awake in my bed. As I lay there contemplating this strange but very real experience in dream state, the manifestation of this future experience had already begun. My first session of this form of healing was 03/02/2022 at 12 pm. I will say this is something that I have heard about and even witnessed, but never felt it was something I needed to have in my life as a form of healing.

I have talked about GinaLynn in one of my previous books, *Coming Out of Darkness.* She has been instrumental in educating and teaching me the ways of our home here. She has given permission for me to write about her, and my introduction to acupuncture, in this chapter.

GinaLynn has been a gift from God. She is kind, wise, powerful and independent. She has suffered ailments leading her to different forms of healing and exploring different spiritual avenues. She chooses the holistic, natural process of healing and is very spiritually connected to her ancestors. They advise and show her signs that could be less evasive, but very healing in natural ways that provide the process she chooses to heal herself.

GinaLynn has her own healer and she calls this woman her investment to whole health and her own personal commitment to self-care maintenance. Her name is Socorro Zepeda. We call her Doctoras Coco. Coco is an endearing name for Socorro in Latin American. Her business is called Salud con Acupuntura (there is a Facebook page); Salud means health. Coco is a Curandera (the word Cura means heal, hence a healer). GinaLynn told me she sees Coco every week, religiously, for what she calls tune ups for her whole health. She says some people invest in spas and others invest in other forms of releasing. She invests in Coco.

So naturally, after this dream, I reached out to GinaLynn to see if her practitioner would see me as I was more than curious to see where this message in the dream would lead me. GinaLynn arranged a time and, God bless her, offered to come and translate my session for me as a mediator. Before I get into the details of my session, I need to state I had no idea the power of this woman before I went. I also had no idea how it would change, mold, release things I had no idea were inside my body. I will tell you that it was one of the most intimate, personal, and whole healing sessions I have ever received.

The appointment was made and set for over a week later and I forgot about it. Prior to the appointment was a week full of new clients. Many sessions interwoven throughout the normal routine of my life with Joe. Our daily afternoon walks, or quiet reading on the couch; just living out life as we do in the new quiet routine we have come to treasure. Tucked in the middle of the mountains that surround our condominium, in this sweet little town. I had no idea that yesterday would clear the old, dead wood and broken pieces that had been long forgotten, hiding in obscure places inside my heart space, but it did. I am feeling something beyond anything I can form into words in this moment. This new freedom of releasing allows me to "walk the walk" from all the talk I have been doing, about the importance of freeing internal space and making more room for growth. I will attempt to tell this story, and this experience, with as much detail as I can.

Before I get into it, I must share this. I have had the weirdest feeling that week. I had a reoccurring dream about a worm in my heart, again, just before I woke up. Sometimes, when I got up in the night to go to the bathroom, I had this thought that there was a long worm wrapped inside and around my heart that extended down to my abdomen. It was so silly that when the thought came, I brushed it away thinking it was a terrible nightmare and to just let it go. This imagery was something I knew could not be physically possible, but also at the time I had not considered the possibility that it could be a spiritual worm. It is important to mention this before I tell you what happened in this session of healing, on all levels, for me. It is also relevant to note that I wanted this woman to have zero information and let her see what she sees in me during the session. Another piece of vital information to share with you is that my heart had been physically hurting me for months, like an actual heartache that is physical and painful. The kind that comes and goes often during the day with a feeling of pressure on my heart at night, when I was ready to go to sleep.

The session:

Joe gave me a ride on the motorcycle to the corner of the street where Coco lives and runs her business. I arrived right on time and when I walked around the corner, her house door opened, and she was in the doorway ready to greet me. I walked into her entrance, we all had our masks on. GinaLynn was sitting on a bench telling Coco she could hear the motorcycle, so she knew I had arrived. I could feel and see her beautiful smile behind her mask. I felt immediately welcome. She led the three of us through her courtyard and into a small healing room. The healing room had a worktable where her patient lays, much like a massage table, or a table a doctor's office would have. On the wall (her husband is an artist) was a huge hand painted picture of Archangel Raphael; it covered the wall from floor to ceiling. There was another huge portrait of four or five guardian angels at the head of the worktable. On the wall to the left was a portrait of a cross with the face of Jesus painted in the centre.

The instructions, prior to the appointment, were to wear loose clothing, stay open to receive whatever happens, and trust all that needs to unfold, will. GinaLynn was kind enough to stay and to keep the conversation flowing, answering questions and giving instructions. She also supplied a clean sheet from her home for me to use on the table because that was part of instructions as well. I was sitting on the chair waiting get on the table, while GinaLynn was telling me that Coco wanted to do a prayer to open the space for my session. I instantly got very emotional, which totally caught me off guard I was not even on the table yet. I got excited like I was about to get the biggest gift of my life. It was a bit unnerving and I wanted to climb up on the table before fear and excitement had a chance to change my mind. I talk about not being afraid and truly most days I can work through the feelings fear can cause, but today it was like a huge war was being fought on my behalf. To be honest, I was not entirely sure if I was ok with a bunch of needles being rammed into my body; and goodness knows, in what places!

It was time for my session to begin, so I hopped up and laid down on the table. Instantly, I started to cry uncontrollably. I mean it was embarrassing for me to be so vulnerable. It was incredibly quiet in the room and when my tears subsided Coco gently continued. GinaLynn kept telling me in English what she was doing and how it was going to feel, when I was supposed to take a deep breath and heavily exhale. She placed all the needles in their positions and her voice was soothing, kind, and strong. My body started to react to the needles. First my heart, it felt like a cool compress was being applied to a heart that needed to be revived, healed, and recovered. Then the rest of my body started to release, release, release. She said that I was blocked deeply by trapped energy that was inside of me, even across many lifetimes. That it needed to find its way so that I could be free to work for God. I do not know how she knew at that point I worked for God, or even that I had authored books, but she did, and I am quite sure GinaLynn did not tell her this about me. GinaLynn respects everyone's privacy and is a beautiful example of not intruding in someone else's lesson or experience. She often sees things and knows that what she is seeing belongs to the journey she is witness too. She leads many of her clients to Coco and then she releases the experience for the person to receive what they are comfortable receiving. I felt a trinity of presence with, and in, the two women who were there to support and facilitate this healing. I had no idea what happened next. It is still with me in a way I am feeling the new life within me. Something long and hard was coming out of my abdomen. I could feel it as I was sobbing and shaking, and my body was moving in my chest, off the table. It was excruciating, and it was fighting to stay as Coco was fighting to release it. It went on for an exceedingly long time, me screaming, fighting, crying and feeling my body being contorted by an energy that did not want to give up its residence. At no point during this experience was I scared, frightened, or even the slightest bit threatened. The whole time she worked, soothed, and prayed in spirit. She spoke in tongues, and it melted and soothed me; I felt angels, Jesus and God surrounding us. Coco never stopped praying, she never stopped loving me, and she never stopped pulling this energy out of my head. At one point I felt very nauseated, but it passed. She stayed with me throughout the whole storm. She stayed in the eye, gently moving this old energy out of me as it was no longer invited to keep residence inside my core.

When I was completely depleted, exhausted and had cried buckets of tears, she allowed GinaLynn to tell me what had happened. She said that there were three energies that were not healthy for me that were taking up space. They could have been there for many lifetimes and they did not want to leave. Their cords were exceptionally long coming from my abdomen and going through my chest. One left through my mouth and two left at the crown of my head. I did not doubt what she was saying because I felt it and knew it was true. I knew she was fighting for me on my behalf to send them back to where they came. She then said she was with Jesus and praying on my behalf to Him in spirit (speaking in tongues). That these energies were laid at the foot of the cross and sent back. She soothed me as she told me all of this while never leaving my side, never taking her hands off my head, never showing me anything but the shining love of God through her eyes. At this point I asked if she had Kleenex to wipe my eyes. I could not express my gratitude for this release with words, I had only tears to shed and she wiped them away. In return I asked if I could put my hand on her heart so she could receive the grace of love through the dedication her work deserves, from Source. She said yes, so I put my hand on her heart and then I asked GinaLynn to come over and I put my other hand on her heart. The three of us prayed and sang together. It was as if three children of God were bound together in that moment of pure spirit unity. A gift from Source to Source.

She then started to take out the needles, one by one, disposing them and I sat up while she did this. She continued to share and answered all my questions regarding what she pulled out, letting me know they will never return to that space they occupied within me. I know that this was exactly what was supposed to happen. This was a death and a rebirth in the most personal way I had ever experienced. I understood that I had to feel all of this to realize my own releasing and the importance of it for my own personal maintenance. I asked Coco for her permission to write this chapter, as I felt it particularly important to share about her. To share my message of healing and share the faith and trust in having an open heart, even when you have no idea what is coming for you. She said with a smile and a twinkle in her eyes "God has already written this chapter." Yes, He had. I just had to be open and channel all the truth. In saying "Yes," you are given new life.

She then made a silent promise to me. It was a message she sent me telepathically! It was, "You have been given to me Tracey as a gift to continue to release your burdens to me so I can lay them at the cross for you. I will work with you even when we are not in session. God has excessively big plans for you and you are not to get in the way of these plans. You will need me, and I say Yes to stay connected to you and the work we are both called to deliver for God."

When I asked GinaLynn if I understood her message correctly, she validated that yes, I did understand she will stay connected and work in spirit with me, as I will also work in spirit with her. I decided before I left Coco that I would commit to taking care of my health in a way I never considered previously, and wanted to be on a maintenance plan, working to release things I need help releasing on a regular basis. I am only here for three more weeks but did book two more sessions with Dr. Coco and committed verbally when I come back next year for five months, I will book a session with her every two weeks. We hugged and embraced each other. Dr. Coco pulled back to arm's length, looked me straight in the eyes and said, in English, "I love you."

I understand that this may not be for everyone, I certainly never, ever before considered this form of releasing for me. However, now I know more than ever I need to take care of things in a way that only other entrusted light workers can do. We are all gifted and have many things to offer others. Helping me rediscover new internal real estate (you know I say this often!) within the literal wall of my heart space which has been opened in a way that I can use the space to create different experiences.

When I left her house, her advice was please rest, quiet your mind, allow the process of your healing to work through the release; eat lightly the rest of the day, and just be. Together, GinaLynn and I walked to the square and then past the church and I realized it was Ash Wednesday. Receiving this gift on this day it became even more sacred to me in a very personal way. We walked into the market, each of us in our own thoughts, bought a delicious juice and sat in the shade discussing things and feelings and just unwinding from the miracle we each received in our very own way. It was during this time out that GinaLynn shared some of her own personal healing journey and how she found, or rather, how Dr. Coco and she found each other, just around the corner from her first home, in the centre of Tequisquiapan. She went on to share with me that Dr. Coco is a tireless healer. She had, through her faith and the power of her love for God, helped many people heal from all forms of physical ailments, cancer, and other crippling things.

After our juice, GinaLynn and I walked around a bit. Eventually, I needed to find a washroom as the releasing had started to process on all levels. Soon after, GinaLynn left to go on to finish her day and I walked to the bus station. Feeling my body unravel with each step, I noticed my heart stopped hurting, I did not feel that ever constant presence and pressure on my chest. Remembering snippets of the session as I walked, I was trying to consider how I should even attempt to write this and then I heard Coco's voice in my head say, "God has already written this chapter." While sitting on a bus full of local people lost in their own thoughts, riding home from the journey of their day, I reflect now about how quietly present I was for them and for myself. I also remembered saying in the session that I cry for so many people and hold space for so many people in my work that today was a day I cried for myself. Releasing, releasing, releasing, out the other end of the needles that were freeing things for me I just did not know how to let go of. The beautiful Dr. Coco, using her body as a conduit to release this energy that was blocking my way, direction, focus and light.

I floated off the bus, walked up the street and noticed Joe sitting perched on a chair, looking out enjoying his peace, his thoughts, and completely oblivious to this newfound freedom that was encapsulating my body, my mind, my soul! I have mentioned before that Joe respects and supports my spiritual work and today was no different. He did not ask specific questions upon seeing me; what I thought or how I felt. Instead, he listened as I said that I booked two more sessions before we leave. Then I expressed my desire that when we come back next year, I would like to see Dr. Coco twice a month for personal maintenance. He said he was glad I told him so he could put this in our budget. That was all that was said between us; it was perfect. We had a gentle, quiet evening sharing dinner with a spectacular view and beautiful sunset. I slept in the arms of the angels deeply that night, healing in the processing and unwinding of all that I had parted with earlier that day. The next morning, I woke, and nothing had changed in terms of my routine. It was same typical Thursday morning externally, but internally I am free in a way that will allow new light into the darkness that was shed yesterday. Smiling now seeing the words that have been typed, thinking, yes, God really did already have this chapter written. I am so blessed by the graces I am granted. Everything, and anything, is possible through trust and faith, stepping out of a comfortable place right into the arms of God. Healing in the grey matters more than I ever even dreamed possible!

KNOW YOUR ENEMIES AND LOVE THEM ANYWAY

This is such an interesting thing to say, but so immensely powerful. Reminding you it is imperative to stay in the middle of any conflict internally, and externally. Knowing your enemies takes time spent in the trenches with people you did not choose to spend time with on a conscious level exchanging energy, time, or space with, yet these types of relationships give you the experience needed in the lessons taught in the receiving of them.

Enemies, to me, are people in your life you wind up with from which to learn lessons. We agree to all the experiences we are having due to a pre-contracted agreement before we even come into this life, in this body, this time. That a spiritual contract is made ahead of being born into human form and while our mind does not consciously remember, our soul does. That is why we react to some people the way we do. Ever met someone who gets under your skin, without any apparent reason? Chances are you knew this person in a previous life and are now meeting again to learn a lesson you were unable to learn, and grow from, before. Some, or maybe many, of you reading this may argue my beliefs, and that is ok. It can be a hard concept to get your logical brain to understand. Some people believe they had little or no choice in being a victim of abuse they suffered. I believe, that without the survival and acceptance of these lessons we would not, nor could not, begin to understand what the lesson has taught us. In any kind of conflict or encounter that appears negative, there is a lesson to be learned. They are not easy experiences to go through; if they were, our soul would not grow from them.

Most of us have gone through a challenging time, one or more times in our lives, with personal heartbreak, bullies, narcissists, or self-inflicted pain. Each of these negative experiences causing pain unto our beings. Depending on the situation, we may not be fully aware of the impact these experiences can have on us or the type of power they hold over us. Believing that we are deserving of the negative experiences causes us to become a prisoner of the experience and delays the understanding and acceptance of the lesson.

This may seem hard to wrap your logical brain around, as oftentimes we are bombarded with outside opinions and other logical answers that help support the reasoning behind this form of pain and heartache imposed by an outside source, person or experience. We experience exactly what we sign up for so we can free ourselves from the aftermath and the toxic scaring.

We can and will work our entire earthbound human life on freeing ourselves from abusive situations. Through many forms of healing, self-help information, physical and spiritual means of releasing, several forms of forgiveness and confrontation. I believe, with my entire being, this is a lifelong process of receiving the tools needed at the exact time we need them to help us continue the healing process of releasing these enemies. In the releasing, we then get to observe the lesson without emotion; providing us the knowledge that forgiving this ignorance and disrespect allows us the freedom and the clarity we deserve. This then allows us to keep these enemies close enough to not only rise above it, but to then be the ambassador of keeping this ignorance in check by the simple state of grace you receive in the forgiving of the infliction. This action on your behalf does not give this energy permission to repeat the ignorance but it does give you (keeper of the gate of your personal space) the lesson you learned a chance to be a lookout for anyone seeking refuge in your heart space. This free space where you have earned the wisdom allows you the healing and education you received as the victim, in turn teaching you a defensive balance. This allows you to choose to take the higher road, thereby raising your vibration of love and light and infecting the darkness that wants to come back into those spaces.

Why would you even want to keep your enemies close you might ask? Good question. I choose to do this because of the valuable lessons I was able to grasp in the releasing of the toxins as a victim. That has allowed me to be a leader in the lessons I have lived and survived through. Knowing my enemies is a great gift. The enemy, most times, does not want to do the work to change their ways, unless they have a life altering moment of redemption. In fact, in my experience, most of these lessons that people choose to dominate fear and force on another is their exact cyclical reaction and repetition. Meaning, you can predict what is coming as most times it is the same cycle of abuse. Knowing this is the way they will continue to respond and try to smooth over and win over others in their destruction allows you a chance to address the victims and offer a safe refuge. Knowing the consistency in this domination of destruction allows you to be the voice in the windstorm, shit storm, tornado, and tsunami. It allows you to stand fearless and in the state of grace in the grey, in the middle, in the eye if the storms brewing all around you. In a world that may seem completely out of control for so many, you get to be in the middle for anyone seeking asylum or refuge. A beacon of constant calm, kindness and peace.

Know your enemies and know them well. Do your research, as much as you need to; go down that rabbit hole and fight for your life. Understand in the deepest part of you what you are having a tough time releasing and forgiving. Sometimes when it is a childhood bully who takes a physical piece of you, causing you deep, dark anger, physical scars as well as emotional trauma and deep dark nightmares can have lasting impacts that create confusion and conflicts in adult relationships. Left undealt with, the pain of these experiences can continue to seep into you, no matter how old you get or successful you become. It seems humanly impossible to not become triggered yourself when a person opens to sharing something relatable that you may have also experienced. We are human and you are going to want to react, hold space, hug, share and even unite with this experience. What I am suggesting is something even bigger than you may have considered. I am asking you to give all of it over, the pain, memories, scar tissue, the experience, the forgiving to your father and mother in spirit. The spiritual parents that experienced the whole thing with you. This energy is a part of you and was promised to you, this support would not leave you. Most of us often forget this when we are born into flesh.

I have witnessed hundreds of life changing moments as people receive miracles when they ask for them. They are specific in asking for what they need, how they would like to release, what they must personally forgive and accept, and the result is the miracle specific to what they were seeking. I mention this because in my experience this is how we release our enemies to the light giving us the clarity, space, and wisdom to know them in all their truth. Forgive them and find a way to love them in the complete releasing of whatever the act of unkindness was, that piece that was taken from us, without an invitation to do so.

In my experience, the forgiveness did not come easy. It was a process, an unwinding of facts, a timeout to heal and to spend time sitting with the events that occurred to really dig deep into the situation. Sometimes legal action was a warranted act of penance, to provide a way out for some of the responsibilities I had as a parent, a provider. We are responsible as human beings for personally providing space for salvation, not only in ourselves (by forgiving ourselves) but also for forgiving others. Meaning that forgiving your enemy can provide an indifference which allows you the time it takes to come to terms with the unwinding of the truth, without feeling the old triggers of the pain that it caused. This falling in line with the facts also allows you to know this enemy deeply and truly, allowing room for forgiveness so you can love this energy in its rawest form.

Yes, this is extremely difficult to do. Most people do not or cannot spend this much time in this raw, burning unresolved state of even trying to find a way to forgive it. Sometimes this takes something as drastic as a near death experience to come back from, so it can help you rise above what you seem impossible to release yourself from. I wanted to write this chapter to let you know that there is always a way out of this darkness, this dank, angry, possessive energy that wants to hold you prisoner, victim or make you a casualty of its war. It is always about choosing and releasing and realigning the new internal space. This energy gained its power by feeding off your emotions. You fed it allowing this energy to consume you or distract you.

There are ways out of every single situation if you choose to see your way out, lift your way out, feel your way out and are open to another way of thinking; beyond the limitations and safe boundaries you have decided to keep yourself in. We all know that growth is about the most difficult experience any human can go through, and along with all growth is a deep pain that accompanies the process. It should not surprise you that most people opt out of growing pains. It is no secret to anyone seeking solace, change, enlightenment, freedom of mind, spirit and body, that the steps are excruciating and lonely. No wonder most people are looking for an easier way to get through all this pain. I believe that when you know your enemies, by name, by experience, by feeling the blows and fighting your fight, not only do you know them because they have no desire to change, you also know their next move, you can feel it. In all honesty, you will know their sincerity, if or when it comes. As you have hands on experience and specific tools that provide awareness. You can offer a forgiving heart, a healing perspective, and a way out of the darkness. When their sincerity is true, they no longer want to be in opposition with you. Thus, creating an opening from your heart space to theirs, a peace offering of love, understanding and acceptance to addressing their broken pieces.

Keeping your enemies close allows you to trust yourself, your loving source of divine white light that surrounds you in all you are, and all you go through. Trusting that this source, somehow in the magic of its inner connection, goes through it with you and that you are never, ever alone in the experience. This is hard when you feel like a victim, with no voice, plain forgotten, feeling isolated and abandoned. I believe, with all I am, that this source rides out every single lesson and bad storm to which I have ever committed. Living in the grey matters to me now more than it ever has. I honestly believe in all my life lessons they brought me a stronger sense of community, internally, than ever before. I believe that things I cannot control externally encourage me to control what I can internally. This makes a difference in my life and in the lives of others I am connected to. So, I challenge you in this chapter to take some time to know your enemies and find a way to forgive the ignorance if you can. Stop judging what you do not know, and accepting what you do know, finding a way to love them anyway. The loving will free you, as well as free them. I am not suggesting you invest any personal energy liking them, we get to choose who we like and trust, I am suggesting the love will release you and your eternal reward is freedom.

CHOOSE YOUR TOOLS WISELY OR THEY MAY BECOME WEAPONS

When I speak about choosing tools, I am mostly referring to spiritual tools. They have a dual-purpose in their knowledge/wisdom, teaching me in their discovery of them, how to share with the people who need them. Along with that is their magic of synchronistic timing. Such as how to listen, hear, advise, or just be silent for another who needs your ears, eyes and presence. I was in the shower this morning, which is mostly where I have come to hear my spiritual source the loudest, and oftentimes I try not to take long showers as the messages can come fast and furious. This morning the message was "How can you lead others to the water so they may choose to drink from its knowledge, if you are not first drinking the water yourself?" Seriously, how profound. A direct missile hit, straight to the core of me. There is so much truth in this. I must first drink, allowing the water to hydrate and awaken the knowledge of what it is I am trying to find in my own healing, using my own tools, and yes, at times weapons so that I can secure and defend what I stand for.

Tools are an incredible asset. In fact, I would not be able to work every day in my life without their objective aid. This is the truest statement, even a form of confession, in saying this. If not for the tools I have gathered over my lifetime, and the experiences that provided me the tools, I could not do my job to the degree in which I am able to now.

Many years ago, I said "yes" to the energy of Reiki, inviting spirit and guidance, symbols, and tools into my life. Stepping out of my routine and stepping into the connection of Source allows tools to just show up! They arrive one by one! The world of meditation also provided tools, grace, quiet, reflection and truth. It is so interesting when you feel confident enough to expand your space, and allow the tools to develop, they do. They find a space to live within you, and the best part of this knowledge is when the ego and spirit come together, defining the best way to make use of the tools. These powerful tools are gifts but also require a matured responsibility to be accountable on how they wield their power. The power of the gift is when you become aware, you intuitively have the need to understand exactly how to apply your gift in the transitioning of the tool you are applying.

It is the most amazing thing to witness spiritual tools in action as they have an essence of their own directive magic, providing anyone seeking the gift a chance to experience a real-life miracle in the receiving. This is where it can become a bit sticky. The magic is attractive, it can even become an addiction in the experience of the witnessing. This can cause one's ego to take on the responsibility of becoming more connected to the outcome of the miracle. To be honest, it is always a natural and spiritual high to be witness to a full-on miracle of healing, clarity, and growth in another. You relate to the person as you channel and/or facilitate what they have been seeking, or looking for, with little or no success previously. These tools at our fingertips that allow us to access and yield power can be extremely hard to disconnect from. In my experience, I have held on to this and sometimes even wanted to share an experience of great worth to others. But honestly, the experience was never mine to share. It has also been my experience to have been on the other end of such powerfully directed gifts, facilitated by other healers and light workers.

In my experience, spiritual tools can range from receiving messages for clients in dreams, one on one sessions, or relaying the message in a hands-on method of being the facilitator or medium. I will elaborate on each. When I am the conduit, or medium, from Source, I am given the ability to provide a direct line of communication to exactly what the client's needs are; often getting right to the core of it. Another tool is the verbal information exchanged in a one-on-one session. Either virtually, or physically, where information is given to me in a thought, vision, or word. Then I reiterate the information and do not filter it in any way. I just deliver the messages and do not even stop to try to reason what the message might, or might not, mean to the receiver. These are spiritual tools that allow the light worker, in this case me, a whole new way of communication that is directed by an energy that encompasses us all. It surrounds us with an easier way to raise our vibration in the hopes of releasing stagnant energy that is keeping us in a position we get stuck in.

How can these tools be used as weapons? When the light worker, or the designated healer you are working with, finds a way to hold you in a place of fear or provides bad advice to gain control. Manipulative power tactics that continue to enable you and take your power away are not tools of true spiritual counsellors. This is a tough thing to witness. As professionals, working for the white light of Source, we want and need to be accountable. It is something we sign up for, an unspoken code of ethics that goes way beyond words. It is just a fact that this work is powerful. We as mature shepherds pledge an oath to stay true to the work and true to the cause and effects the work may bring to the people who contact us. They are seeking the tools to discover another part of themselves, they needed help and direction in pulling out their tools. As agents for the white light, we need to stay in the middle using the tools we have been granted to provide, or help awaken, the healer seeking the healing. If we abuse this power, the tools then become a weapon and the weapon can cause a diverse reaction to the person receiving the healing.

Please be responsible with the tools you are gifted. Take inventory, cleanse them, protect them, and keep them tucked away in the sacred places you cherish. If they are crystals you use, build them an alter and share them with Source. Learn what is needed in order clear and cleanse them. If you do not know, ask Source to provide the information you seek to secure them and care for them. Ask and direction will be given to you. Trust this is how the cosmos works. Take care of you and your beloved tools and they will provide all you need to grow yourself and lead you in the direction you are meant to go. If they are visions and dreams, you may want to write them down in a sacred place to honour them. Doing this will allow you to reference the information you have received. If the message is not in clear upon receiving, taking time away and reviewing the information you have been given will be interpreted in a new way, realizing the answers you have been seeking have been provided. Gifting yourself with expanded growth.

Mediation is a tool as well, and for me, it has provided many journeys for myself and others to travel to places in my mind, beyond what I ever dreamed possible. This tool has expanded and lifted the limitations I put on myself when I am facilitating as a medium, channeling for others. I receive personal, private messages to questions they are asking during the meditation. When you say "Yes" to Source and to a client, you then get to soar with the meditation directed by Source which is gifted to the receiver. It allows me the faith to get out of the way so Source can step in. I just get to be the deliverer of the message. This is beyond humbling, as repeatedly it is about the client receiving what they ask for, but more importantly, about connecting consistently to the need they require. I have been hired to facilitate guided meditation work by clients who need assistance in connecting with Source. Quick, fifteen-to-twenty-minute guided meditation sessions. When first hired by this client, I was extremely uncomfortable instructing these sessions week after week. I was having the hardest time trying to figure out how this could be helpful for them, or unique with how frequently we were together. I just gave it up to Source and said, "You know what your child needs. I will just get out of my way and fully trust you to deliver the messages you have for your child." I was just the messenger. Again, I want to elaborate these tools you will be receiving and recognizing as power tools need to be handled with care and always put away in a safe place when you are not using them. The tools themselves yield power and carry a great deal of personal responsibility. Awareness, accountability, honour, and respect that the tools do not belong to you but come from Source which entrusts you with the power they wield. If you use them in a selfish way, or in a way to gain access to the power you are trying to acclaim, possess, or steal from another, the tools then become a weapon.

Of course, we have free will. We were given that as a gift from our spiritual heritage, our birthright our re-entry to this life when we decided to become human. In my experience, Source will not intervene unless called upon. I do know that we all live the lessons we choose and the choices the lessons provide in the choosing of them. So, it settles me to know we are having to address each lesson in the transitioning back to the light we come from. I do not really call this Karma anymore; I call it fate and truth.

CHOOSING YOUR TOOLS

Tools of any kind are, by their very nature, useful. The technological world around us is mind boggling to me. The advancement of humankind and the capabilities that have been developed over the last fifty years have brought exciting inventions with endless possibilities. We have tools to help us regulate our body functions that we can wear on our wrists! At our disposal are tools to help us with anything we can think of. These tools are teachers, aids, and advisors. Now is the time to dream bigger than you ever imagined. Evolution is a natural part of life and there were enough creative minds who have always had this knowledge that the world would explode with the ability to share all kinds of information in, numerous ways to access it. It has been the process of growing pains and maturing in and raising our intelligence to meet the demands of the sound of the world and what the world needs to continue its quest for more.

The past three years has halted, stunted and shifted our state of clarity, with some of us asking ourselves these questions: "Is a fast-paced life better than the uncomplicated way life used to be? Is this compulsive need for grander, bigger and easier ways of doing something a better to live? Or is sometimes the slower labour of love and self-satisfaction just as important? Is there a way to capture and harness both the speed of this growing artificial intellect versus the need to remain a participant with living human intelligence? Is there still room to combine the reality of our technologically advanced world and the importance of old ways, so that both sides work together and stay in the grey?"

These are certainly the questions that have rolled around in my head, and in my dreams during sleep.

Last night I dreamed that I was actively involved with moving mass amounts of dehydrated food and smoked meat on a convoy, with many moving vehicles carrying hundreds of volunteers to Ukraine. It was so real I could smell the smoked links of sausage in the crates being moved into the line of trucks. In this dream I was beyond frustrated when I finally arrived only to be turned away at the borders. We were turned away because the Government had not been a part of the acceptance of this gift of love. There was too much red tape and resistance. I woke up in a room where my hands were tied together by pieces of white sheets binding me, holding me in a place I could not move. I could still hear the starving people who were dying. The tools of offering were so close to help so many, but the greed just allowed the dying to continue. I woke up with tears streaming down my cheeks; my heart was so heavy. Not long after I opened my eyes and in a thick sleep-filled voice, I started to tell Joe my dream. In a sad, rhetorical explanation, he shared his thoughts about the dream. I could hear the heavy sadness in Joe's voice, teaching me about the politics I try to avoid and not involve myself in.

Prayer has become my biggest and most powerful tool. Especially for moments like this one where there is so much emotion, that I am left feeling raw. It is hugely offensive to a soul who only wants love and healing for the world she lives in. Sometimes I use it to scream my pain out, knowing it is going to a place that understands that what is upsetting to me, and may not be my business. This energy does not judge that; this love just holds me until the wave passes. Prayer has become my secret sauce, my hope, my truth, my connection to something bigger than I ever imagined. Prayer is my heart and voice telling my truth from the internal place it was stuck inside for so long, trapped. I had no idea the power of prayer until I started to really use the tool, define it, claim it, and make it a personal piece of my existence. Prayer, for me, is not always done in the traditional form we associate with when we think of praying. Sometimes I am intensely discussing with Source what I really do not agree with or understand about a situation. Prayer can be lying in the arms of my divine spiritual father, brother, mother, spiritual source having a much-needed cry; the kind you have, when it is over, you have the hiccups that slowly lull you to sleep so you can recover and heal. Prayer has become the most personal, practical, efficient, ever ready, and most easily accessible tool in my entire soul toolbox. Prayer is my mediator, advisor, mentor, best friend. I do not have to wait for a special time or place to pray. Prayer for me is an instantaneous action, any time and in any place. I pray as I wait for the water to boil in the pot, cooking the potatoes. Prayer heals, advises, teaches, brings forth miracles, allows a connection of hope, and truth. Prayer for me is communication that sustains the reality of my existence. Prayer is my voice being heard, songs being sung, praise being directed to the respect that my spiritual family deserves.

Prayer is the love language that Source uses to connect with us. I have grown in this tool as it guides me to a place of acceptance naturally, easily. Prayer remains embedded in my whole existence. Prayer is my favorite go to tool; it softens the edges when it is necessary for me to do so. Prayer has many layers. Meditational prayer an intent to sit quietly offering time as a tool. In an offering of holding space for Source, lost loved ones, spiritual guides, or angelic energies. Guided meditation is something I practice regularly with people who ask for recorded sessions from and with me. If guided mediation has been requested as part of my healing session with a client, it is reserved for the last fifteen minutes of our time together, separated from the healing part of the session. I step out of the way as Tracey and my body is a vessel guided by spirit. When this happens, I assist in painting the view for my client. I describe what I see and what I feel as an extension of the meditation that is as personal for me, the one channeling, as it is for the host who is being gifted the meditation. People who receive this form of gifted prayer rely on the meditation in their own ways, listening and revisiting the meditation often, gathering its treasure, or the personalized messages the meditation provides for them. I have been told many times there are no words for this type of meditation and that I should do more of it for others. My thought on this is that God always sends me exactly what I need to offer in the asking so I do not seek it out, it always lands exactly when it should. I say "Yes," and then release it.

According to spirit law you can have anything your heart desires. I really love this. There is something to say about this, right? It states you can have anything your heart desires, but what it does not state is the price of the desire. If the desire is not something that will assist your growth but feels good to indulge in, you will have your moments of living through the intentions and the lessons you felt you needed to have and experience. I know now that when you choose the desire you need to have, the desire will play out in all the actions that caused the attraction of the desire in the first place. I have also learned through this acceptance of the desires, you experience big highs, big lows, and usually land someplace in the middle of all of it. Desire is yet another especially important spiritual tool that teaches you what it is you asked for and how to expand from the desire you were inviting into your being. Prayer is my way of reaching out to the spiritual family that has not only taught me that they never left me, but they show up for me. This two-way conversation shows up during my day, dreams, life, bringing an abundance of signs, warnings, teachings, and sometimes hard conversations of what I need to dig deeper at releasing, and coming back to meet them in the centre of my being. Yes, all by using this powerful tool I call prayer. Spiritual communication is my most personal, powerful tool.

Crystals are tools I use for different forms of protection, awakening, healing and soothing. Crystals can and do show up to work on what they are directed to work with. Through their power, their gift represents a loving, non-threatening intervention. Crystals are born directly from our mother earth as that is where most of the crystals, I share with others, come from. I say most, as some are directed from other sources beyond our solar system. All crystals, in my experience, have their own unique blueprint of designated healing properties. I have been using crystals more personally for about four years now. I have been gifted many crystals, and as many as I have been gifted, I have given out as gifts, spontaneously in session or in conversations about them. I just know in the moment what crystal is best suited. I get the message from Source as to who needs what crystal, what it offers and why they need to own it, for as long as they need it. Oils, Palo Santo, candles, religious articles, rosaries, crosses, and angels are also part of my toolbox.

Part of the power in receiving and then gifting your most precious worldly treasures, is to be honoured at the gift and the presence of the gift someone took the time to not only seek out, or feel called to gift you, but the thought and the sacrifice in purchasing it for you. The receiving of this spiritual aid doubles, or triples, the power it presents to you and the time it takes to help in supporting your healing. But also, like all of us in spirit knows, when paying this gift forward repeatedly, it never stops manifesting. I used to get very emotionally tied to the worth of the gift when I knew it was expensive, as well as powerful. I now realize it cannot be all powerful if I hoard it away, like the greed of Gollum, from the famous Lord of the Rings. I must decide to let it go, all of it; well, most of it. I still covet my master sea foam Andara crystal, which I use as a tool in session daily. I feel like it belongs to a piece of my heritage, my lineage. For me, it is as important as a sword is to each archangel.

I was gifted a huge round piece of lithium, a purple, flat crystal. I remember receiving this along with a few others a couple of years ago. These handpicked crystals have been used in many sessions over the last three years. I loved them enough to treasure and respect them enough to release them from my possession, to be free to do what they are called to, on to the journey they need to be on. I can tell you when I am called to give something I treasure, it is always a tiny struggle for me, of letting it go. That feeling leaves as quickly as it presented itself because the purpose of it is to continue the path that is directed to be on; this living energy has a mind and desire of its own.

Such is the case with the lithium I was given two weeks ago. The lithium was the last crystal to leave me. I did use that crystal in many sessions prior to gifting it last week. But the call to gift this crystal to Laura was bigger than the tiny resistance of coveting and keeping the crystal. Laura needed this more than even I understood. She received it, felt it, and held it to her heart before we tucked it under her pillow during her session. When she left that day, after her time here healing the deeper levels of her heart, she smiled deeply and hugged me tight and went on her way. In Laura's words after receiving the crystal, "I continue to process my healing. When I feel the heaviness and the darkness clouding around me, I pick up the crystal holding it to my heart, allowing the crystal to do the heavy work releasing what, in that moment, I do not have the strength to release. This crystal somehow has the strength to release the weight for me. When I could not process the heaviness, the crystal had the power to take the lead, teaching me that the pain would pass. The simple gesture of holding it made me feel as though I was not alone in this loneliness."

The second time she came for a session she talked about sharing her lithium, Betty. She told me she was invited out to a gathering and truly did not feel up to going, but something (Betty) pushed her to reconsider the invitation. She ended up going, causally showing up. That night she met a new connection, and she was immediately aware that this person resonated with her frequency. She felt it from the first time she saw him, it was a warm invitation for her. It took a little while sitting by herself, but a little later in the evening this person, who exuded kindness towards her, sat down with her. Laura realized, as this was someone, she felt a connection with, that she could trust and share pieces of her with him. Not long after, they were sitting across from each other, in deep conversation of mutual trust. Laura then decided to take out her lithium, sharing the gift of its power with him. As he was holding it and feeling its vibrational energy as well, he asked her if she realized how powerful the lithium was. She passed it around to a few others who were present, so they could experience it for themselves, and then she tucked it safely back in her pocket.

This example of the power in using crystals represents, in its living essence, it is a piece of magic. This magical tool is helping her brain calm in the storms she has been addressing, sorting, and fighting. At the very same time it is also available to help others by touching it, allowing their own healing to process to begin. This crystal was born to heal, to hold, to advise, to love and to help slow down the noisy activity of abuse, absences, emotional misunderstanding that can, and do, cause anxiety. The power in this crystal quiets your mind, allowing your spirit of love and peace to join your brain in the fight for silence. Thank you, Laura, for giving me permission to share something so personal with so many others who are trying to find their way through all this noise. Your courage in sharing may help others to take the chance they deserve, finding the peace they need, to find the happiness they crave.

In several of my writings I have mentioned the power of words. It lives in the timing of the delivery, the sting of the accuracy and the truth that words reveal, as they shower down around, and through us. Words have become one of my most favorite tools to share with my soul. In hearing my own voice and giving me space in silence, sometimes chastising me for moments that my words were harsh or intended to hurt. Being aware of the words escaping me allows me to hear truth of my voice, the voices I present in truth to others. Words are special. What we say affects us, it affects the energy around us, and within us. Recently I have learned to back down, back off, and rethink what I might have suggested or said initially, or without thought, especially in the heat of a triggered, passionate moment. We all know that once the cascading damage spews from this space and our voice echoes the thoughts that escape us, it can create sometimes permanent damage. Once these words are spoken, they cannot be forgotten or taken back. The damage can sometimes be lifelong and life changing. Our words are the representation of our truth in the way we think, act, and view situations. Our words can be used as weapons or feathers depending on the way you intend them, striking or soothing. Words can create miracles or disasters, all with various levels and degrees of tension or intention. When words in turn are morphed into action, or an acting upon what was said or suggested, they can have catastrophic consequences. Words are worth the forethought and the thinking ahead of being spoken, for with the power they wield, they can change the outcome of any scenario. Words can and do heal, they also bruise and break hearts. Words are a tool you may consider taking more time to sit with, ponder, write, and roll around in thought before saying them. This gives you extra time to shift your energy. You might even decide to reconsider, or rephrase the verbal agenda and the passionate trigger or fire you were caught up in. Trust me when I share that this is always personal, we as humans always want and even need to voice what we believe in and hold pledge too. Sometimes the words need to be considered before they are out and cannot be recovered. Words are a tool, sometimes overused, but never overrated. Words are the core of your power!

JOINING THE FORCES IN YOUR NEW VIBRATION

Those who are already awakened, and have been in the process of awakening, recognize the frequency to which we are awakening. The hum of the vibration is different. It is as if you can hear and feel the vibration of it. This higher sound and energized intelligence allow us to address what we have become aware of. Fully understanding the emotional triggers that keep us bound and stuck, instead of free from them. Releasing these triggers frees us to explore a different reality. It is like we get to separate what was exhausting and depleting our power pack, our sacred internal voice and sound, of what we know as our truth. The memories are still fully intact of the lessons we choose to experience. This memory teaches us the difference and stops you from repeating the lesson and returning to the feeding ground of emotional chaos that kept you addicted to the lower frequency energy, the density, and the confusion that was able to drown you in its wake.

Most of the population is not only not open, but are also in avoidance, or full-on denial, of this truth. Why? Because if they know that this truth is their reality, they will have to do something about how this truth makes them feel. This can morph into change, uncertainty, pain filled anxiety, loss of control, loss of personal power, mostly feeling they have zero control over the outcome of what they do not currently have faith in, the future outcome. This manifestation of full-on truth and acceptance in oneself requires growth, challenging work, honesty, acceptance, accountability, and a fair amount uncertainty. People would rather stay safe than find their true, whole self.

Arriving at the belief that these valuable nuggets of knowledge are true, reveals to us that we have truly awakened, arriving at a higher frequency of existence. Knowing this truth allows you to understand why it is important to awaken and, in time, you come to realize that the heartache is lessened, if not completely gone. Your raised vibration has bled out the toxins with all the energy that was destined to leave your vessel. What is left within you is the residue of an extremely healthy awareness - that what used to lay you up, or even take you out, and knock you down for sometimes days, moments, or hours, is no longer the case. What is left is very meaty feeling of indifference to a situation that might have previously pulled you in to one of two directions.

Let us just take a moment to ingest and digest this word indifference. When I looked up the definition of this word it states that indifference is "the absence of compulsion to or toward, one thing or another," "a lack of difference or distinction between two or more things." The synonyms for indifference are "apathy, casualness, complacence, disinterestedness, disregard, incuriosity, incuriousness, insouciance, nonchalance, torpor and unconcern."

Because this is my new tool these days, I am often using it to help one release this old energy that held so much power within the person. I use this new word and new tool to define the result, indifference. When you look up all the meanings that the word indifference suggests, it reminded me more than ever to agree to living in the middle of grey compliance. The grey is a place I can choose without the state of emergency of my emotions dragging me away, as a form of distraction. The grey slows me down enough to realign and reconsider all the scenarios of power building in and around me, vying for attention. Of course, I have common sense kicking in as a number one source of the commitment I have made to be safe and keep others in my circle safe. This is the grander picture of the meaning of indifference from a soul learning and raising your frequency perspective. Indifference allows the time out required to not be addicted to the trauma, drama, or outcome.

Until we learn this higher intelligence, where there is no need for superheroes, we will not stop seeking this instantaneous fame, recognition, or the power that makes one feel invincible. That others simply could not live or function without our interaction, connection, or lifeline. When we rise, up and out of this narrow-minded thinking, we are then able to be one with the same energy that resides within, co-creating the one source of love we seek to identify within our own selves and the connection of source we come from. There is simply no longer the need to be heard and acknowledged on this grander external scale. We just learn that indifference is our new source, answer, and resolve to everything and anything we need to expand on and with.

Of course, there are two sides to this, and the other side would be a cool indifference related to the calm warm kind of indifference. The cool side would be working without the state of grace, or the state of love involved. As you are finding your truth in this word you will discover how the work feels on both ends of the spectrum. The warm will find you in the gentle state of truth, sadness, concern, opinion, ultimate forgiveness. The cool indifference will leave you in a state of heaviness, narcissism, revenge, judgment, and a wanting to hold on to this and hurt, or judge, for an extended period. Thus, allowing the lower frequency who is invited to a banquet to feast upon you, for as long as you hold on to the cool indifference seeking a justice that is just not even possible. Do not underestimate this enemy that knows you and has been invited to the table inside your being. You have had conversations with this enemy discussing the anger of your own injustice and the injustices, and carnage, you witness. This enemy knows you personally and subliminally invites, seduces, and suggests the sweet taste of bloody revenge. This enemy that lives off your anger has a very vested interest and counts on you to feed it with your lower frequency desires. Never, ever underestimate the energy, it will invest in you to lure you back to the place and space you gave to this energy. If you have escaped its clutches, it will fight for you as your light grows bigger. You become more seductive and desirable to it. This is not said to instill fear, it is just factual. You have the secrets and the tools, as well as your very own distinctive power to conquer it. You just need to say, "No, no thank you; you're not welcome, please leave."

When you make a commitment to join forces, and I suggest you take this very seriously, you work from a space that allows you the freedom and the decency not to just have a voice but to be understood. This meeting and coming together in this vibrational awareness generate a healthy place to grow forth. Creating stability and communication that is more internal than external. If you take the time, energy, and patience to understand the dynamics of this vibrational living energy, with an intelligence far beyond your ego comprehension, combining your aged soul's experience, you have ability to join these two forces together with all the lessons and wisdom they bring with them. This all comes with growth of the awareness teaching you all the truth you never considered. This new power tool provides the ability to become even brighter in your flesh than you imagined possible. Use this new power in a way that will serve you in a wholeness you have yet to even discover within the walls of your human consciousness.

I have started to practice the art of loving indifference. It is so interesting to me that the warm meaning of the word indifference this has been teaching me to soften my delivery to the external world I am in daily communication with. This loving indifference slows down the core of my internal need to be armed with a weapon. One that I may have gone to fight battles with several times in my past. A defensive state of being on guard and deflecting oncoming pain in a traffic jam of trauma and drama. I am quick to defend what I have worked so hard to build and what I have worked so hard to defend in myself, and in my personal circumstances. Living in loving indifference allows you a healthy, emotionally disconnected perspective. It allows you to consider different opinions with loving kindness and whole perspective. This allows you to detach from defensiveness and aligns you with endless possibilities. Newfound freedom in the witness of what used to challenge, consume, and absorb you into a state of attack and defend mode. This loving indifference is the key to extinguishing fires that consume humankind with loud voices, loud actions, and loud solutions. Reminding us that common sense and kindness spread so much easier when applied with a loving indifference and a compromising solution. This way everyone gets heard and has their own stake in the game and the way the game is understood and followed through on. Loving indifference is non-confrontational. It has a power source that is indestructible. It is a constant, energized source of enlightened power that never goes into sleep mode, it is always there to remind you who you really are and where you truly come from. Again, as a reminder, cool indifference is cruel, has an agenda, a bitterness that comes from a frequency that wants to rule, control, manipulate and consume power; yes, your power.

HAVING A VOICE MATTERS

Having a voice does not come naturally for some people. In fact, most people, when it comes to sensitive and personal matters of the heart and soul, want to clam up and divert the uncomfortable and often emotional conversations. These are ones that need to be addressed if you are seeking true self love. Having a voice is necessary in the world. Most people, if given a chance or an opportunity to talk have many things they would talk about. The voice I am referring to, the voice that matters here, is the sensitive, often pain filled side of you that you keep secretly tucked away in the deepest parts of your solar plexus.

People love to talk about the way they see and feel and experience the world. In the work I do, it is common for people to possess a deep yearning for them to know their future. They have many questions. Where it is going? How it will affect them? Will they be successful? Will they meet their true love? How will that turn out? What will be the outcome for their retirement? Will they have enough equity to sustain a healthy, fearless existence? I have found a way that serves a purpose to explain to everyone who comes to me both new and reoccurring, that I cannot really predict the kind of session you will receive from me. I can tell you that it will be your own unique experience. I use my voice to talk about my gifts and the work I am called to do by explaining that my experience and wisdom comes from me working for Source and help people work their way out of hard, emotional spaces. The experience I have gained has taught me how to work mostly on releasing past scar tissue and resolving stubborn, antagonizing, lower frequency bacteria that has found a space within and is in no hurry to move out.

I use my voice through becoming and allowing, a personal channel (or medium) as a physical agent for Source, to help others also release what they have no idea how to get unstuck from. They know they are stuck because they have voiced this; they even know what it is that is keeping them detained or a prisoner of the war that battles on within. They just do not know how to have the faith and trust required to shift and release the particles keeping them hostage.

Finding your voice is the first step in true self-healing and reconnection, providing your voice the power of hearing what you need to release and relating to the reasons you are doing the work, which will align a healthy future where you have your power back. The work I concentrate on the most is teaching people how to address the past and release the depression and suppression, fear, and restrictions the lower frequency has possessed and locked them into. Finding your voice is like truth serum and when it is confirmed by a healer facilitator using their own voice, matching the power of yours, it is the magic in the healing miracle that brings enough force to release this unwanted agent from your body.

In my sessions with clients who are seeking healing, I face this energy most often with the client providing a vocal invitation for me to enter her/his space, as a conduit for the energy to pass back and forth between client and Source. There is an exchange, a conversation with the energy on a soul subconscious level. This conversation builds courage, as the person tells his/her truth in the experience of voicing and communicating things they felt they were not able to do in person. This brave conversation gives them the courage to face their personal demons. For example, the abuse they may have suffered on all levels. This voice is the power tool they most often find in a session, as they discover the shifting and the releasing of past trauma/drama. This allows them to feel the effect of the work done by the healer and the ego inside of them in their session. The voices shared in this sacred space, from client to Source, of the confliction allows a healing to happen in a way the client has not experienced before. Therefore, it is so important to allow time to heal in between these intense sessions. This is spiritual surgery, and it requires time and space, and love and peace, allowing room to heal internally.

More times than not, a visit from a loved one is present in the healing session. This visitor sometimes walks right in with the client (in spirit) as if they have always been an appendage of the person who is here seeking refuge. Sometimes there are extraordinarily strong messages and even visual aids that I receive, to make me aware that my client is not "alone." One time I was hosting sessions in a store in Lexington, Michigan. A man came into the store with two friends. It turns out that these friends, two young women, had dared him to do a half hour session with me. He was clearly not really interested in this kind of healing, exposing himself and being vulnerable, but he took the challenge and signed up. That thirty-minute session turned into an hour session of such intensity for him, that it changed his perspective and his direction. His father walked into the session with him in a lumber jack coat, knee-high boots, and an axe. This young man was absolutely in a state of shock when I described his father, and what he was wearing, in complete detail. He was visibly shaken and had to sit and digest this. His father had several messages for this young man.

This much detail does not always happen in a session but most times if there is a message, I voice what I see, smell, hear, and share the message with the client. Again, using your voice matters and it is your responsibility to share what you are supposed to share and release it after you share it. When you decide to use your voice as a tool to help soften, educate, share, advise, refer, consult, defend, as a platform, either one on one, or in a crowd, you will feel the message and the energy in the way that your voice and the vibration of your truth resonate. Accountability is established in presenting your truth, with your power and your words. You will have a different connection and the effect during a virtual session is a whole different dynamic, energetically speaking. Using your voice in these days and times is more powerful than any other time on this planet because of the constant changes, which offer little or no consistency or stability. We have the means, the wisdom, the historical archived evidence that now, more than any other time, our world will be saved by the word and the actions of humankind in general, as well as a whole.

If you choose to stand tall and constantly check in on the relationship between your ego and soul, your words will become the action. You will follow through on consistently presenting a way to have a new, normal form of stability, creating the structure, that every single person deeply (even without the knowledge) craves. We crave the result of any conflicting lesson. We crave the deep need to be heard and the deep need to be loved. We will be fed this fuel by the words around us that becomes the action of what we are craving. Choose wisely, consult your heart and soul in constant conversation and counselling, collaborate and discuss with this internal counsel of wisdom what your next words will be. Following up on the words in the action of them will help you to move through the next lesson, or connection, which comes into your space. I have said this over and over, repeatedly, until it has become habitual knowledge for me. Words are the most powerful tool you will ever have in your toolbox.

LOVING FROM THE CENTRE OF YOUR HEART

I want to start this chapter with expressing a deep gratitude for Jackie. She is someone who has practiced healing and coaching work for several decades. Jackie is soft, yet firm. In our exchanges of loving energy, while working through places that desire another perspective, she helps me to identify a different outlook. With this knowledge, this new voice can then be put into action. Jackie's logical genius allows an opportunity to be heard in a way that is so personal, you cannot help growing in her wisdom. I feel like we are partnered by Source to help delve deeper into the tools we need to exchange, try on, and develop, in and for ourselves. As a result, adding to our own ever growing, ever exchanging tools. Sometimes when a particular challenge arises, we work together at sorting it out and the releasing around it. It has been a complete honour, with sincere gratitude, to work with this gifted, caring, charismatic spirit, and fun person. Jackie's energy is endless, loving, compassionate, fun, and kind.

We were discussing something, a year ago, and I distinctly remember a shift in my heart as I heard her softly say, "Tracey what I hear you saying is this…." I audibly heard her say it, but it was more of a shifting internally, like she made a point to say, "I heard you say this…." This sentence, the timing, placement and the context was so powerful, I forgot my chain of thought and what I was trying to say and stopped to listen to what she heard me say. Can you believe this shifting is so simple and elegant?

It was kindly presented in the context of the moment, shifting the perfect timing for source to ignite source, delivered from one human vessel to another. "What I heard you say" is a tool I use so often, these days, it travels with me from moment to moment and from exchange to exchange. I have become so invested in this "What I heard you say" mantra that it has become far more than words, it has developed into an action of pure hearing.

I hear the words align in my brain and form, it is like I can see them forming, but I hear them internally. When I am deeply absorbed in a session, I have noticed that I have been closing my eyes on purpose to stay aligned and in tune with the sound and the words coming from a client who is deeply, passionately, committed to expressing their truth in a very secure space for them to speak from the deepest parts of them. I hear them saying what they need to say and then I can reiterate what they need to hear, in what they have just allowed to surface. They are heard, sometimes for the very first time. This human being feels safe enough to talk about what they have not ever before felt safe enough to rise above and out of them, in a way of fully confronting, and accepting, what they have to say, and how they needed to express it. This new tool has tempered my ego, allowing the slowing down of what I feel needs to be expressed and allowing another to express what it is they believe will allow them access to a new space yet to be developed, in the middle of their own heart and soul space.

Bringing me full circle to the title of this chapter. This past week I had yet another opportunity to work with Jackie. We sorted, congregated and aligned our sources to be what each needed them to be. Jackie ended the conversation by saying, "Sending love from the bottom of my heart...." and then she stopped and changed the verbiage and said "...from the centre of my heart space." This stopped us both in mid-sentence. Living, loving and healing from the centre of your heart space, for me, means that I am not loving from the bottom or from the top. This means that I have found a way to fully encompass the truth in this statement that Jackie so beautifully and elegantly presented and orchestrated in her own use of the powerful statement. This was beyond anything I had ever visualized, and everything I wanted to materialize, in the full circle of what this means to me. When I reached out to ask her if I could write about observing and experiencing this personal shifting, in the whole dynamics of the timing and the energy encapsulated in this gift, she responded by saying this. "Yes, absolutely you can use the phrase "centre of my heart space." I trust it was for you, and your book it is not a statement with which I am familiar. It just came through. In leaving you the message, it dropped in."

Isn't this just like Divine Source? To just drop into the centre of our hearts exactly the way, and as gently as, this whole timing and message did. Isn't it just like Divine to use simple elegance, class, grace, and persistence to continue to have the most profoundly, perfectly executed timing for words that mean so much? This example of grace in this interaction and deep connections with others.

This newly coined phrase is wrapped around my heart space. For me, its significance means living fully from the centre of my heart. This means that some days it is going to rain. There will be days that are going to have a heavier energy and some days are going to be busier than other days. This means that I am constantly being distracted and pulled away, and sometimes pulled apart. Regardless, I get to choose to live and love from the middle of the space of my heart, soul, and healer within. For me, this means that I will be less bothered by the elements and the lack of control I have around what is happening. In turn, I will have more control of how to not only accept that I have no control over, but that I have a deeper consideration and knowledge of the frustrating confusion around all the fear related to the energy that seems distorted. Again, it is not personal unless I make it personal. I get to stay in the grey, in the middle, in the centre of all living life and all energy that surrounds and supports the world I am living in. I get to choose, and in the choosing, the clarity lights the path so I can see all obstacles in my way.

Living from the centre of my heart, soul, body, and mind

is a change within to rise into this private, loving space that has always been and will always be. It brings balance to the healer within, the one that wants to be heard, accepted, and unconditionally loved. This soft, sweet spot in the centre of me is also in the centre of the Divine love that has always been and will always be there.

Today I had this beautiful moment of being in both worlds at the same time. I was morning musing with Dana. It was a gentle, loving exchange and at one point, a message from her Sam, for her, came to me. It was beautiful. Sam was chatting away and I was giving Dana the messages. It struck me funny that at the exact same time we were talking, I was deboning a cooked chicken. I know this sounds strange in the context, but the message was so beautiful. I was trying to multitask. I wanted to make Joe a delicious chicken sandwich for lunch and I wanted to give the onions and the mayonnaise time to blend their flavours, for a few hours together in the fridge. I was delivering the messages from the spirit of Sam to Dana, and right in the middle of the message I said that I was deboning a chicken, without the reason. I am sharing this with you, so you can see the context as profoundly as I did. Dana also got the same message, that this was the moment of truth. I was living in body and flesh so effortlessly without stepping into spirit, and out of spirit into body. This was the combination that both are as real and as important as the other. I was oneness in spirit and body at the same time without separating and disconnecting. Oneness in delivering a message and being human, totally present for both. At the exact same time, in the moment of clarity, Dana and I got this huge shifting of total acceptance and totally living from the very centre of my heart space.

I challenge you to try incorporating both for yourself. Take them on, try them on, see how they feel, fit, and how they align in your beautiful being. The truth is you will love them as much as I do and use them both just as often. We are all looking and seeking new ways to develop self-love care, a way to feel loved, accepted, and worthy. Remember "I heard you say.... I love you from the

centre of my heart!"

THE POWER OF
GREY GRACE

Move over, at the table in the centre of your core, and make space for everyone at your inner core table. We are less than whole without learning the valuable lessons we are meant to learn and teach each other. Please understand that it is an invitation of love. When people invite you into their internal world, it is to help make sense of something that for them may be out of order. The first awareness in a scenario like this is to understand you are being called upon in a sacred trust as a lifeline, a guide of hope. This energetic cord becomes a living lifeline of unconditional love, a connection from Source relayed through you. You say yes to the state of grace and become an appendage with Source, together as one. It is effortless, sustainable, and supportive as the base becomes the holding tank and anchor.

This brings us back to something I have previously discussed in this book, indifference. I have discovered there are two kinds of it, warm and cool. As mentioned, I have been learning how to incorporate and genuinely express what this means in my daily life, and with clients, as I have become more aware of its power in the past few months. This new, advanced, tool that I have a whole new awareness about, when used in the moment and for the context in which it is intended, teaches me anything beyond my own experience of healing and growing over the past several years. Loving indifference is just exactly what it sounds like. This indifference allows me to love and understand the complexity of all situations without being fully, emotionally connected. This may sound impossible but trust me when I say it is not only possible, it is imperative for growth, peace, joy and fulfilling happiness.

Attaining this habitual mindset for me, I had (and still need) to address every single emotional trigger that connects my response to every action that directly or indirectly invades or involves my living daily moments. I will elaborate more on cool indifference in this chapter. When I take something unnecessarily personally, I notice I get aggressive, defensive, ignorantly opinionated, negative, distant and cold. I call this energy, just so I can name it for awareness purposes, a cool indifference. I disconnect from the world, my self-love and I feel the darkness settle in and congeal, like a layer of destruction and carnage around my heart. It is like an actual crust starts to form, like acid has been laced around my whole internal space and it starts to corrode. Pieces separate and break off and the cool indifference leaves me in a state of full-on loneliness and judgement. I feel desperate and cut off from myself. In this desperation I get louder, needing to make my point of justice and feeling my truth; that discovering of this truth is the only way and the whole truth. I make little or no room for another person's point of view or any other course of action, except the course I believe in. This cool indifference puts my body in a state of paralyzed aggression. Not only have I stopped thinking clearly, but I have also stopped seeing clearly. I have stopped speaking with clarity and I become an aggressive, defensive bully. Cool indifference is a very real state for me, and it does not have one single thread of grace at all. In this state of cool indifference, I have started to notice my heart is heavy and full of pain that gets stuck in the arteries and clogs my freedom. I have noticed that I am able to break free so much quicker than ever before because I have recently been able to learn the difference between cool indifference versus loving (or warm) indifference.

The first step in this awareness between these two choices is when I notice the heartache and choose to love instead. The heartache is gone, it leaves the moment I choose to raise my vibrational energy and choose to love instead. I feel the shift immediately, teaching me the power that the loving indifference makes. I still get to experience all the things the lesson is teaching me, but the difference is I step out and allow Source to step in, cloaking my heart with a shield of love. This teaches me to not feel the struggle or not have a need to go into defense mode, or even feel the familiarity of pain that a personal attack might have triggered; a negative emotion looking to feed a negative lower frequency attack. This is something I have started to incorporate in my sessions and am trying to teach others how this works; how to choose this mindset repeatedly in their everyday journey of enlightenment and clarity. Living in the middle of the power of grace can teach you the consistency required to stay in this grace.

The power of grey grace is so soft, you barely notice it is presence. It is consistently aware of the difference between love and control. Love has no room for control, possession, power wielding authority, nor the need to be seen, heard, or even right. Grey grace is strong and soft at the same time. It has a wisdom and strength that is silent. An awareness that cannot be seduced, purchased or is even active in any game seeking revenge, or a win in the direction of individual power. I find it interesting that loving indifference allows me the room and freedom to see the entire picture play out in and around me, both with an internal versus external perspective. Grey grace is just noncompliance in a loving energy that is uplifting and frees me from the attack and defensive position I have lived most of my life in. There simply is no need to defend what is already secure in the centre of my being, which allows me to practice grey grace in every single moment I get to be human, having a spiritual experience.

The secret sauce to acceptance is awareness. The awareness adds the spice of knowledge in a way that you start to crave loving indifference. This the neatest part of living in the grey grace you choose to stay in. You start to taste the bitterness of cool indifference allowing you the opportunity to choose love. When you choose the power of grey grace you get to stay in the middle and live in the middle. You truly learn the way, means and power of compromising. But the biggest gift is you truly learn the personal gift of taking things that used to settle into your heart, soul, and can release these historical triggers. The kind that could plague you and your surroundings for sometimes years, months, weeks, and days. Sometimes you can release in the exact moment you are triggered by someone else's need, ignorance, or lack of kindness. Even if you are a victim living with a spouse, or in a relationship where this is a perpetual cause and effect of the ignorance, or the lack of growth in the other person, you have the power to step out of the way and stay your course in the middle of grey grace.

Grey grace is an earned credential that you receive in the elevation of advanced soul school. This is achieved when you become what you say, by taking action on the words you speak. I believe, with all my heart and soul, it is worth the investment to secure this habit as a daily, sometimes moment to moment, awareness. Are you going to be challenged? One hundred percent. Will it be worth it? One hundred percent! Living in the state of grey grace is one of the most blessed things you will experience in the advancement of fully living in the freedom and grace of the middle part, the centre part of your whole self.

THE QUIET WORLD
OF GREY

Fewer words create a bigger space for power. What is interesting about this is that the more you grow into this quiet space or what I started calling a "quiet world," the more powerful you become. I will try to put into words the feeling I am trying to describe to you. It is a feeling of security and warmth. The feeling of a presence of something that cannot be seen by the physical eye; an energy that understands me. I feel this presence holding me in my quiet world and it makes me feel less lonely. There is a familiarity to me, of how it feels to stand alone in the flesh versus standing alone in spirit. The air, the energy becomes so thick and rich and saturated with a presence that allows me the world of support from where this source comes from, energetically. It is so rich, mostly because it does not need words to make it richer. It just becomes this way by its mere presence and the acceptance of its existence. As a shepherd for Source, this richness allows me the room to receive. By talking less, I absorb more.

I want to talk about a recent shift I have noticed and for a couple of weeks I was trying to find a way to work through it. This was hard for me, but I have had some time to sort it out and put it all into perspective. Joe and I are winding down, taking longer weekends and shorter work weeks. It started in Mexico at the beginning of the year. Joe has grown beyond his hobbies that caused him long hours of scratching his head and cheering on the sidelines. He is more ready than ever to move on from daily work and find other things to do with the time that he has generously given to all the others who he felt responsible to guide, teach, instruct or help. He has also been feeling the years of wrenching and building things for others that have taken its own wear and tear on his body parts. Together we have had this plan for a while, to slow down and take the time we want, to discover what we would like to build the rest of our lives around.

We have been trying to find other points of interests that engage both of us. Some people let go of material things and find they need much less as they get older, multiple cars and items of clothing, as examples. I like the sound of this, but, it is a bit uncomfortable, realizing by slowing down, you have more time to just "be." For me, this time equates to a lot quieter moments to fill with productivity. Yes, it is strange to say but I find it difficult to get used to having this time to do whatever you want to do. Read a book, go for a hike, sleep in, have a late breakfast, go golfing, go for a walk or drive by the lake. It almost feels like you are playing hooky out of your real job. The job that you were used to for the last forty years. I hear people say now, what I said for the last ten years, "I can hardly wait. Oh lord, I just have 5 more years and then I can retire, my pension kicks in, I will have my life to live my own time to fill in the moments, days, hours. I get to be free".

Free from what? I say to myself, now that I am here and I am not even fully retired, only semi-retired. I feel this empty space that I have a desperation to fill, sort out, align, stimulate, and retrain. We are all creatures of habit, so when I tell you that the new shadow of quiet sneaks in to create new noises in your ego, this is a fact. It causes my brain to make things up in my body, and my body and my brain argue these facts. The quiet is loud and sometimes it is even louder than my own heartbeat. This free time takes time to get used to as well. For years we run from this quiet, mostly because it simply was not available or even an item on your daily menu. Meaning you could not order it at all because it was on the section of the menu labeled "Senior Specials." Most of us do not think about growing older or even what it might feel like when you arrive on the red carpet and get to have the benefits that come with the lovely grace of growing older. It is the silence that has, in some surprising ways, been the most intriguing and challenging for me.

I was out with my baby sister a couple of weekends ago, on a day adventure. She came up to the lake, where Joe and I spend our time in the summer in an RV, situated in a nice recreational community. We took off in her little red truck without a plan. Our only mission was to go to a huge flea market near the lake. She is 7 years younger than I am, so she is not sixty yet. Still a young, vibrant, full of energy nomadic soul. Jacqui is fun, spontaneous and free flowing. She is wise and loves to manifest all kinds of beautiful things, through action, the power of words, and by loving in a way that allows her to take things less personally than most people. She is a chip off the block. I suppose we still and always will, teach and remind each other what unconditional love and gratitude not only mean but stand for. She challenges me and when she asks a question, she truly really wants to know what I think about what she is asking me. She makes me smile just thinking about her. She is very thoughtful and truly kind. She brought me two gifts that day, as she knows I am going to my best friends daughter's wedding, and I excitedly shared with her the dress I found for the wedding. She went online because she heard me say I wish I could score a cute pair of daisy earrings to go with the pretty dress. She found some earnings and ordered them. The centres were yellow with white daisies. She hand-painted the centres black and painted shellac on them and gifted them to me. The other gift was more for Joe. I have a tattoo that he, loving, refers to as "the blob" on the inside of my right ankle. I have had it a very long time and it is not very pretty; I must admit. She bought me an expensive bottle of cover up so that the day of the wedding it will not show. This is what I mean about her, she is incredibly thoughtful. Hard not to love every stinking day, hour, and moment I get to spend time with her. She is cute, spontaneous, and fun. She reminds me to be kind, as she takes the time to care.

We were out walking the strip in Grand Bend, and she stopped to pet a big dog and chat with his owner, striking up all kinds of conversations on our way. We ventured in and out of stores and I just watched her interact with anyone and everyone she walked by. My silence was in the observation of my sisters need to connect, interact, converse and ask personal questions, as she really took in and listened to the things people were sharing with her. What I found the most interesting, and even a bit disturbing, was I was not interested in any of the conversations my sister was so absorbed in. In fact, I honestly was a bit annoyed that she wanted to ask so many personal questions that really did not seem to be anything I felt she should be asking. That was a huge moment of awareness for me to step back, step out, and step aside in what was important. In those moments, to those people, my sister making a connection was something they needed.

Wow. That realization was a huge bruise to my heart and my ego. Let me try to further explain this as my heart and ego stayed bruised and at a standoff for a couple of weeks, as I tried to sort out my feelings. Firstly, why didn't I care? And secondly, why had I felt so isolated and so disconnected? I have always prided myself in being aware and knowing what I have always been good at. That is, knowing what people need to hear, how I can support another person, how I can stay connected to and for them even if it is at a distance, but still holding space for anyone who needed anything. I was second guessing my goodness in this space. I was second guessing if I was tired of being considerate or was I snubbing a person and disconnected in my actual interaction. In truth, it was all the above.

As a human being who has spent sixty-five years on this planet, I have come to know that all the above emotions and elements came face to face that day for me with my sister. This deep thinking has allowed for some even deeper soul searching. After asking for some spiritual direction from one of my favorite mentors, Dr Wayne Dyer in spirit, it is safe to say I understand that it is just ok to be whom you are in the moment. You get to do whatever it is you are doing. It is ok to be present; it is ok to not be present; it is ok to stand tall and profess all the truth, passion, gumption and life lessons, within your own space speaking to your own soul. Ask your spiritual team, for whatever you require that allows you growth, perspectives, awareness, internally or externally. Whether that spiritual team is call Source, Mother Mary, Jesus, angels, guides, past loved ones it doesn't matter. What matters is asking for help and staying quiet to receive it.

When you realize you are feeling something that does not sit well inside of you, then your awareness is kicking in and is coming to the middle of the grey matter, in the centre of your being, where you need to spend time. It was in the spending of this time over the past two weeks sorting, letting go, holding on, recommitting, realigning and forgiving myself for not feeling the things I used to think I should feel. That understanding illustrated for me, my huge personal growth and the strides I have made to spend my personal time in a way that I have not spent much time in discovering. Uncovering new ways to heal and hold space with a loving indifference.

I used to be that person that needed constant interaction all the time and now I know that healthy timeouts do not hurt anyone but allows me a newfound energy to revisit what does need time and energy. Also, interesting to note, there is still a hollow space that sits right under my chin and stops at the bottom of my heart. This is like a piece of vacant real estate that I talk about in other chapters. I am very aware that it is there; empty, clean and free of clutter. It is a tad uncomfortable as I feel like disconnected, as I have not connected yet. Something grand and wonderful is going to move into that space and it is going to spread God's love everywhere. This is a space that is making room for way more miracles and way more magic than I could have ever dreamed possible. I know it is big, mostly because growth is always uncomfortable, unpredictable, and requires the deepest amount of faith you have yet to discover. Blind faith and the manifestation of unconditional love has zero agenda. Meaning bags must be packed, without question, always.

WHAT DO YOU DO WITH ALL THE FREE SPACE?

This is a question I have been asking myself lately, sometimes more than once a day. What is the free space I am feeling between the bottom of my chin to the bottom of my heart? Why am I having a very hard time identifying what it means and why it even feels empty? It feels like something is missing but in time I have been able to identify what is it. Can you guess what the answer is? It is all the things I used to think mattered most and it resided in that space. This has shifted for me and is either grown up and out or completely gone from that space it occupied. Thus, leaving a gaping hole. This hole was filled with things, memories, decisions, choices, relationships, examples, noise, structure, obligation, routine, and procedures that kept me in that place that hummed of distraction and duty mixed with responsibilities and accountability. This is what I have been fearing in a sense, of not bringing meaning to my life or needing to be needed in a way that was so important to me for many years. I think to myself, is this what happens to so many people who have been lucky enough get to be my age?

I guess if I am thinking this to be true, some of it must be. But it is deeper than just old age. It is the awareness that now is the time to continue to do what it is I have been able to share with the world and put it into some sort of consistency and act upon the words. It is a time of putting "my money where my mouth is" and be the things I say and say the things I want to become. I always wanted to find a way to soften my words and bring them into a place of powerful action. It has taken me this long to figure out the exact formula of not too much adding, just a sprinkle of this and a touch of that. It has taken me this long to learn the art of listening and the art of repeating the message back to the person who just relayed it. It has taken me this long to practice the art and the power of breathing and the different forms of healing available that apply to breath work. It has taken me this long to step out of myself allowing Source to step in and relay the love that Source has for his beloved. It has taken me this long to understand that space is the most important gift you can give your mind, your body, your being, and all the people around you, who grow deeply from the gift of space you allow for them, as you live with and through them.

This freedom of space not only allows you to grow it is also a gift you extend to anyone else you are connected to. What we seem to take for granted is the quiet gift of space, but it can help others grow in a way we do not even take the time to consider, in our own growing pains.

What do we do with all this free space? We continue to grow, nurture and heal within so we can recognize the gift and then find ways to share it with others. If we are invited to join another in and on their own healing journey, that offering space, or holding space, is something that is a key ingredient in the offering of your space in the first place. Hold space, listen, be aware of the struggles and the work that another person has decided to take on. Listen with love and interest, compliment and remind that person how far they have come. Help the other person understand that they are not and will not ever be alone. Remind them that they have lifelines and other options, both externally and internally, to lean on and lean into. We are a community, and we do and will find our own source of external and internal resources.

How can we share this healthy space with others? We must first find and remind ourselves that this is something we need to initiate and agree upon claiming and sharing this space. However, we cannot share what we do not know or have not given thought to. So, take this time to wallow in the internal emptiness. Feel how it feels even if it is uncomfortable, take the time to feel it. Ask yourself why it is uncomfortable and what you need to do to fill the hole. Spend time in the uncomfortable, quiet state that makes you feel unsettled and question the "why" and "how" to fill this space with the work and the things that sustain, feed, and fill you up. You are the only one who knows you, besides Source. You can work quicker with Source and spirit if you invite them into this big empty space.

We all grow in the quiet pockets that this life provides us. We all need to step out and step into another quiet dimension that is being offered to us where we can. If we are quiet, still, open, and wise, we can hear the ancestors of our linage speaking to us, our guides assisting us, and signs from all the assistance of the angels we call upon, who truly and deeply want to help us reach our true potential. This team of unseen supporters, (for most of us, felt and heard by some of us) are our biggest fans. I believe when we achieve, they also achieve like any team that is committed to a common outcome. This team is, for each of us, our biggest cheerleaders, watching over us guiding and us to completion. Silence, although uncomfortable, is a way to connect not only to this source but to your own internal power.

Keep busy in this silence planning, manifesting, creating, and allowing yourself timeouts without feeling guilt or obligation. This is a particularly good point, when I first started having time that belonged to me and not to a timeclock or a paycheck, I did not allow myself to think too far out of the box. Over forty hours a week owned that space, that time and I obliged doing the job that paycheck mandated from me. This was my routine for over fifty years, I was contracted to do the work, adhering to responsibilities that allowed me to plan for the life after work. This is where this gets interesting. Everyone, including myself, thought retirement was going to be like a honeymoon vacation. I caught myself waiting for the day I could give up and say, "Yeah! I am retired and my time is my own and I can do anything and everything I ever dreamed possible!" Well, it was a surprise when it was here for me and I still felt incomplete. I felt lost, and I felt guilt. Yes, hard to believe but what I am telling you is the truth. The work world I belonged to for so very long had turned me into a person that only felt worth if I was being productive, producing money or working at a task, a service to others. For myself it was a process to work through the quiet pockets of time after all chores were completed in my morning and the process was to take small timeouts of quiet to sort out all the clatter in my brain.

I am not fully retired. In my profession now I get to set my own hours, but I am on call for Source. I do tell everyone that I work for Source, and this is my fourth career, but this is my most favorite. I am called to work for Source, so in some ways it is my karmic contract getting to end my human life this time, employed by Source, helping anyone who reaches out. After every session I have started to say aloud, "God, you make the most beautiful children. I am honoured and happy to serve you and them." Your last chapter should be full of life. You get to choose.

Be ready to feel the shifting that does not sit right in you. In this silence it is usually something you pushed down deeply because it may have made you feel too uncomfortable addressing it. Let it rise into you and your consciousness, identifying itself and use your life tools and guides to release it, making room for new self-awareness. The free space this creates internally is your new power tool, a gift to use, to choose to fill the space with what is specific for your life lessons, journey and experiences. The more open you are to new space to plan and manifest the more successful you will be for you. I often say if you can stay in a place of self-love and self-awareness then you will naturally heal, not only your own being, but every single person that meets you will also find healing. This is very factual when you become the love and acceptance of your grace. You will exude grace as you become a living magnet of God's love; your inheritance shines through and in this quiet you are whole. Meaning, the world heals just by you expelling your energy. Your power is precious and if you take this seriously you will make a difference just in your presence alone.

I will end this chapter by saying it is sometimes hard to

fathom why humans choose so much emotional pain, conflicting scenarios but, it has been my observation we do. I think and I can only share from my own pain filled journey, I want to get through as much as I can, forgive as much as possible, and work through all the scenarios because honestly if I learn the lesson in it, by the grace of God and life I may never have to repeat it. If I can grow to another level of enlightenment in the lesson and the healing it provides, I will be able to understand the meaning behind the pain filled lesson. This really makes sense and is the truth to me. It also makes sense to me that if I am uncomfortable with silence there is a ton more lessons to learn in the space and the gift the quiet is providing me. This quiet forces me to look deeper into the pockets I shoved aside or buried down, acknowledging in the silence that now is the time to address the uncomfortable feelings within them.

LIVING IN THE MOMENT MATTERS

Living in the moment matters. Make room at your table for everyone, choose to live in peace and harmony. Forgiveness is a gift to cherish and to understand its power. This power wields the key to success and whole self. Remember this always, we are less than whole without connections; it is how we learn from each other. As humans we need both worlds to explore and both worlds will teach us the balance of living in the grey, that it matters more than anything, and it will teach you everything you need to be successful in life, love, matters of the heart in personal relationships and matters of compassion in your living essence. Balance is key. Be spontaneous, be kind, be thoughtful, be loud, forgive someone/something every day and spend time in reflection.

We choose our lessons. I know that most of us, myself included, want to blame life circumstances on the course that life has taken us on, the personal choices made on our behalf we had no control over. The ignorance in the choice's made by others in charge of our destiny, or education, from infancy to the time we started to make choices for our own well-being. Our state of mind depending on what those choices led us to have some rough roads or patches to work out, compromise on and solidify, creating our destiny, again, of choice. I believe in every circumstance there is a lesson and I believe in every lesson we can sustain substance, clarity, and growth.

Here is where we can really make changes for the betterment of whole self. I believe in second, third, fourth, and even in an infinite number of chances to get things right, in order, and in place within oneself. I believe we never ever stop living in lessons, so in saying this we might as well get comfortable and settle in. I have really come to understand the secret to success, for me, is to believe that I get a new chance in every second I am aware of these moments, of living fully in my presence and state of presence. I have just stopped trying to find my next fix, my next happy moment, my next high, my next peace, my next conversation. My reality is just being present in my state of space, my state of mind, and the joy my body knows it is addicted to, by living mostly in this euphoric state. How do I do this? By truly living in the moments, I get to live. Being fully present in them, and making those moments matter by awareness and practicing gratitude.

This takes commitment, concentration and training. It is almost related to the physical boot camp that people advertise to get your body fit. The mental clarity as your body becomes, and adapts, to the vigorous routine you have begun on; this journey of wellness to train your body into this new habitual routine of exercise. What happens to your body when you introduce this new method to the muscles that have stopped functioning on this high alert level? They remind you that you are causing them pain, and sometimes it takes a few days to adjust to this pain. You will also notice your body does not like this pain, so it adjusts quickly to strengthen and support the new routine. Your internal body works this way by mentally releasing what it is you have been harbouring, justifying all your behaviours that are not healthy for you. Your new mental adjustment, by feeding it positive endorphins, will align with your spirit and your soul begins to align with Source. That creates a new, positive adjustment to your wholeness - body, mind and spirit. The meaning behind this is to understand that our whole being wants so badly to take the easy way out. It is my belief that a very large percent of our population would rather take the easy way out of not wanting to do the hard work and lonely self-commitment it takes to become whole self-sustainable. We are not wired naturally to manage pain, so we avoid it as much as possible.

The secret is to walk into the pain. Allow the time, energy, respect and love that is earned by working through these hardships. Be accountable, responsible, learn what it means to love yourself enough to fight for all the things you desire. The key here is to spend some time knowing what it is you truly need, want, or deserve. Identify the things you truly need and what you think you might need and realizing those are two entirely different things. When you know what it is you need to experience you then release the request, time and time again to Source, pleading your case in the lessons you requested to learn in the first place, before you were even incarnated.

We are on the clock in these vessels of human form and flesh. Do not settle, ever. Fight for your life and fight for the experiences your life has an opportunity to explore. Find your grey; find your wealth; find your soul; find your mind and settle all the things that keep sabotaging your happiness. Find joy in every single, solitarily moment you get to breathe. When life finds your body failing, find peace and lessons in the quiet your body needs to recover or discover where the next journey might be taking you. Sometimes that journey is right back home to start another life all over again. Find peace and acceptance in all you are handed.

Make the most of every moment. You get to find what it is you are searching for and what it is you have yet to discover, there is no shame in any of it. There is only life yet to discover while you are in this vessel. Be brave, patient, kind, and choose love. Be wise with all these gifts. In all ways remember to forgive yourself and others time and time again. Make this your healthy, habitual habit. The rewards of this practice go far beyond anything I could ever suggest. Please believe me when I say this has mattered more to me than anything, to remain in a state of forgiveness!

Living in the moment matters. Staying in the moment matters. Healing in the moment matters. Growing in the moment matters. You are all worth this incredible knowledge of self-discovery. I will spend all the time I have left on this earth investing in love. I will personally invest with anyone asking a question so that I can help direct them in self-discovery and self-love. You are all worth love.

I have also learned that loving can mean quietly holding space for someone not ready to take on this mission. There is a definite boundary in not knowing everything; I used to think I had all the answers. I do not, only you know what you need.

Living in the moment allows me the kindness to understand this difference. Living in the grey matters. This grey matter has taught me to stay in the middle, understanding that everyone deserves to be where they are, learning to be their best and worst selves. We all host darkness. It needs to be honoured, respected, completely compartmentalized and contained, so we do not lose one more beautiful day. This commitment to self gives you permission to continue the path of your own healing in a healthy, systematic way.

This grey matter has taught me to both stay strong and stay soft. This grey matter is where I encourage you to live, find, recover, and discover living in this healthy space. You are all you have. Make every moment count. Your life depends on it.

Tracey Pagana

www.ingramcontent.com/pod-product-compliance
Lightning Source LLC
Chambersburg PA
CBHW072146090426
42739CB00013B/3295

* 9 7 9 8 2 1 8 0 7 3 6 7 1 *